FACING DOUBT

A BOOK FOR ADVENTIST BELIEVERS
'ON THE MARGINS'

REINDER BRUINSMA

ISBN 978-0-9935405-2-3

Copy editing: Jonquil Hole, Crowthorne, Berks (UK)
Cover design: Mervyn Hall, Alphen aan den Rijn (the Netherlands)
Lay-out: Pre-Press Buro Booij, Maarsbergen (the Netherlands)
Printing: Lightning Source, La Vergne, TN (USA)
Photo author on cover: Studio Klaas Norg, Medemblik
(the Netherlands)

Contents

Preface

This book has been written by a Seventh-day Adventist for Seventh-day Adventist Christians. But it is not an official church publication, nor is it published by a denominational publishing house. In fact, I did not even try to have it published through one of the official church channels, even though in the past my books have usually had the imprint of one of our Adventist publishers. But this book is different and I know that it would be difficult for those who decide what is acceptable for publication by an Adventist publishing house to give the green light for this book— even if they personally would like to see it printed. I appreciate the opportunity to publish it through the Flankó Press in Binfield (UK).

My special target in this book is a segment of the Adventist Church that I will constantly refer to as 'believers on the margins.' I have written especially for those in our midst who have doubts and concerns, for those who wonder where their church is going, and who have trouble believing as they used to.

I make myself vulnerable here. I will be quite open about the fact that there are many things in my church that I do not like; that I also have many doubts and unanswered questions; that I am critical of some of our church leaders and of trends that I see and the direction in which major parts the church seem to be going. Some may not like this, but I am ready to take that risk, because I believe that what I have to say could be helpful to many doubters in our ranks.

The manuscript of this book has been read by a number of friends and colleagues, who have made many useful comments. Their input is much appreciated. As always, my wife Aafje has read the MS and weeded out some typos and helped me to improve the text. I am grateful to Mrs Jonquil Hole, who once again was willing to copy-edit one of my books.

On the surface it may appear that I am quite negative about many things in my church and that I am pessimistic about the church's future. That would, however, be a wrong conclusion. I am not about to give up on my church but I try to take the long view. I believe current clouds can blow away and eventually new winds can begin to blow. The last thing I would want to do is discourage any readers by my analysis of the crisis in Christianity in general, and in Adventism in particular. I would be devastated if my book drove people away from faith and away from their church. On the contrary, I hope with all my heart that it will help at least some readers to take a new 'leap of faith' and then (re)-connect with their church.

I have written this book because I deeply care for all those who have ended up 'on the margins.' I do not have the illusion that reading it will make all doubts disappear. I do hope and pray, however, that it will help those who read it to establish priorities in their faith experience and in their ties with the church, and dare to live creatively with their uncertainties and doubts.

Zeewolde, The Netherlands
Summer 2016

CHAPTER 1

Staying or leaving?

I have now been retired for a number of years. But I have, at least up to this moment, remained quite active. I continue to preach in Adventist churches in many different parts of the Netherlands, the country where I live, and occasionally also further afield. I continue to teach seminars for pastors in various countries and to participate in many church events. And I continue to write, which brings reactions from far and near. My weekly blog[1] is regularly read by at least a few thousand people around the world, and this, in particular, has made many aware that I tend to be quite frank in what I say about my church and my faith.

Sometimes people will say, 'Now that you are retired, you can, of course, be more open and say things you could not say when you were still an active employee.' There may be some truth in that, but I have—throughout my life—been rather outspoken and have never tried to hide what I think and who I am. This does not mean that one can always say everything one thinks, everywhere and to everybody. Honesty does not equal foolishness. I have always tried to act responsibly, but also to be true to myself.

That today, more than in the past, many Adventist church members tell me of their concerns about current trends in their church, and express their doubts about their faith and about specific traditional Adventist doctrines, is partly to be explained by the fact that they perceive that I am willing to listen to them without condemning them, and that they feel that in many ways we are kindred spirits with similar doubts and concerns. But this is, I believe, not the only—nor even the most important—reason. We must simply face the fact that the numbers of people who have difficulties in accepting current trends in their church and who feel that they can no longer subscribe to everything they were once taught as the 'Truth,' and no longer sense the relevancy of much of what is going on in church, is steadily growing.

It would be tempting to describe in detail some of the stories that fellow Adventists have told me in the recent past. But I do not want to betray the trust these people have shown towards me. I want them to read this book, but I do not want them to recognize themselves in what they read, nor fear that others will recognize them. The Adventist family may be quite large, but at the same time it can also be surprisingly small and I am always amazed at how many people know each other.

Many of those who have spoken to me, or have sent me e-mails or Facebook messages, or have contacted me in other ways, have told me that they are going through a crisis of faith and that they find it impossible to continue to believe in God or at least in many of the things that they have been told about him. Many of those who are well informed of what happens in the church's organization and about the viewpoints of some of the top leaders, have lost all respect for the higher echelons of the church. Others openly wonder whether or not they want to stay in a church that seems to be becoming increasingly conservative and fundamentalist. Concrete issues such as the role of women in the church and the church's attitude towards gays and lesbians are real stumbling blocks for numerous church members in the Western world—and not only there!

I am not prepared to give up on my faith and I want to remain part of the Adventist Church. But in this book I will argue that the Adventist Church is in a crisis of major proportions and I will not remain silent about the many things that bother me in my church and about the doubts that affect my personal faith. To make clear what I want to say, I believe it is, first of all, necessary to paint a wider picture of what is happening in Christianity in general, since—in spite of what some may prefer—the Adventist Church does not exist in splendid isolation but is part of—and susceptible to—trends in the wider Christian world.

THE CHRISTIAN CHURCH IN DECLINE?

We must accept the undeniable fact that in today's environment the Christian church is not doing very well. In fact, in many countries numerous church buildings are being auctioned off and church communities are either dissolved or fused in an astonishingly rapid tempo. The Roman Catholic archbishop of Utrecht, a major city in the Netherlands, recently predicted that in the next ten to fifteen years one thousand churches (or two-thirds of all churches) in his archdiocese will have to be closed![2] Cardinal Timothy Dolan, his colleague in New York, announced that nearly one third of the 368 parishes in his diocese will soon be merging or closing.[3]

Many of the traditional mainline churches are in deep trouble, but, on the other hand, some other Christian movements are doing remarkably well. The modern Pentecostal movement has grown from a handful of converts in the early 1900s to a worldwide army of hundreds of millions of believers, or, according to some estimates, to almost twenty-five percent of all Christians.[4] Much of that growth is taking place in the South, or the so-called developing world, but charismatic Christianity has also cornered a significant part of the shrinking Christian religious market in the Western world. There is every reason to believe that the Pentecostal religion, with its emphasis on religious experience and relationships *('Do you love Jesus? Yes, I love Jesus!')* rather than on the minutiae of doctrine *('How do you define the human and divine natures of Christ?')*, also attracts many postmodern people who are in search of a religious shelter. The postmodern person who turns to religion will usually not primarily seek intellectual stimulation, but will first of all be looking for an experience that involves his entire person.

At the same time, there is a paradox, which, at first sight, is difficult to understand. That the church in the South tends to prefer a rather conservative and fundamentalist expression of faith may not be so strange. But a significant part of the Christian church in the West that manages to survive is on the 'right' side of the theological spectrum or is gradually shifting further toward the 'right.' This may be most visible in the United States, where 'the religious right' has over the years been very strong. However, in Europe also a fair number of conservative churches have grown—including many Pentecostal churches—while most of the more liberal denominations have seen a steep decline. Must this perhaps be interpreted as a kind of protest against the postmodern easy-on-doctrine-attitude and against the permissive tendencies in much of contemporary Christianity? There is apparently a segment of Christians who want to be part of something they feel is truly worth belonging to. It has been suggested that many of the mainline churches do not, in fact, lose their market share because they ask *too much* from their members, but because they demand *too little*.[5]

But while some denominations are gaining strength, this is definitely not true for the Christian church as a whole. And there are many reasons why the institutional church in the Western world has declined.[6] Postmodern people tend to look at the historical record of Christianity and wonder why the followers of Jesus have done so poorly when it comes to walking in their Master's steps.[7] They see a history of religious wars and bloodshed, of deadly crusades and vicious inquisition. They see a tradition of oppression by members of the clergy, who were often extremely successful in lining their own pockets. They notice the frequent internal controversies in denominations, the bitterness in theological debates, the religious hatred and bigotry. They have noticed the endless fragmentation of the church that Christ intended to be one. It has not gone unnoticed that many church leaders gave a far from clear signal when, in the 1940s, the Jews were rounded up and shipped to Auschwitz and to other places of unmentionable horror; when church authorities sided with the privileged class in exploiting the poor; and when many white Christians found biblical arguments to defend slavery, racism and the inhuman *apartheid* policies.

Small wonder that the church lost so much of its credibility in a large part of the Western world. Small wonder also that many find it difficult to trust and respect Christian congregations and clergymen, in view of the fact that Christians so actively participated in the atrocities in Northern Ireland and in the genocide in Rwanda. More recently, the numerous cases of sexual abuse in the Roman Catholic Church have further eroded the credibility of the church and its clergy. But before Protestants succumb to the temptation to feel morally superior when hearing about these Catholic scandals of the recent past, they should remember the rather juicy tales of the sexual escapades of some of their famous television preachers. And a little digging shows that Protestants also have their own skeletons in their ecclesial closets.

STAYING OR LEAVING?

The few preceding paragraphs provide a sketchy but very disconcerting picture of the negative reactions the church must face in today's world. But in spite of everything that happens to the church, many Christian men and women are still happy with their faith community. Their church is and remains a major part of who they are. They continue to be active, volunteering huge amounts of time in the life and operation of their congregation. They are generous in their financial support for the program of their home church as well as for missionary and humanitarian projects around the world. They attend church services, often more than just once a week. They read their Bible faithfully and regularly, buy religious books and DVDs; they watch religious programs on television and listen to religious music. They talk to others about their faith and invite people to join them for special church events. *They simply cannot imagine life without their church.*

So, yes, there are numerous Christian believers who definitely want to stay with their church. It is not something they have to be persuaded to do, or do because they lack the initiative and imagination to consider other options. They stay because they want to stay!

There is, however, an ever-growing army of Christian believers who have left their church. Most denominations report a constant hemorrhage of members—of men and women who have drifted so far away that they can no longer be considered church members in any real sense of the word. Church officials in many countries report growing numbers of people who have consciously decided to request that their name be removed from the church roll. Some leave because of some bitter personal conflict that has remained unresolved. Some just fail to re-connect when they move to another town or to another part of the city, or after having experienced a serious breakdown of family relationships. Some decide that what they hear in church is no longer relevant to their daily lives, or find the life style expectations of their church too prescriptive and unrealistic. Others realize they can no longer agree with certain doctrines. Some move away from the church but still consider themselves believers. A few move away from Christianity altogether and embrace a non-Christian faith. Thus, there are all kinds of reasons why people leave their church.

Lots of young people who were brought up in a Christian home and went to church with their parents, go their own way when they become teenagers or adolescents. Many parents who still find their faith and church allegiance important must face the, often traumatic, experience of seeing their children choose a different path. In the mainline Protestant churches in the United States only thirty-seven percent of young people stay with the church.[8] A study conducted by the *Barna Group* found that only 1.5 percent of Christians between the ages of eighteen and twenty-three have a truly biblical worldview.[9] This is another way of saying that the younger generations have by and large become thoroughly postmodern. This, to a large extent, explains their lack of interest in being part of, or remaining in, a religious organization.[10]

This is not to suggest that church leaving is an issue that only concerns young people. People of all age groups are leaving, including even retired pastors, sometimes after a church connection of many decades. And many new recruits to the Christian faith wander away rather soon after their 'conversion.'

Church leaving provides a challenge for Roman Catholics as well as for Protestants in general. But Adventism is not exempt from this trend, although it is only recently that the Seventh-day Adventist Church seems to have awakened to the fact that its retention rate of new members is quite abysmal. According to Dr David Trim, the director of the Office for Archives and Statistics of the Adventist Church, forty-three out of every one hundred people who are baptized leave the church again within a few years. He also reported that in recent years the Adventist Church has had to 'clean' its records and 'dropped' almost six million members between 2000 and 2012, because they simply were no longer there (and this did not include deaths). From 1965 to the end of 2014 some thirty-three million people were baptized and became Adventist church members. In that same period thirteen million of them left the church.[11] These sad figures do not include the hundreds of thousands of young people who grew up in the church but decided not to be baptized, and who, rather sooner than later, just slipped away.

'ON THE MARGINS'

Staying or leaving? For many it is a dilemma they have already resolved. They stay because they are happy and feel fulfilled in the church. Or they leave because the church is no longer important to them, or has actually become something very negative for them. For many others the situation is far from clear. One could say that they are *believers on the margins* of the church. They are on its edges. Many hover near the back door. They are still in, but wonder for how long. Or they are just outside, but still are well aware of what is happening in the church, and wonder whether perhaps they might at some future moment move inside again and once more become active church members, or perhaps sit somewhere in the back of the church.

There are different reasons why people, often almost imperceptibly slowly, move towards the church's back door. They feel increasingly uneasy about things that happen in their local church or they grow ever more weary of some trends and decisions of the denomination to which they belong—or both. Or they wonder more and more about the biblical basis for particular church doctrines. Some feel increasingly hedged in by the life style demands of the church. Others simply do not get along with some of the key people in the church. Others again have gradually begun to read the Bible in a way that differs from what is officially fostered as the correct approach to Scriptures, or even doubt the very foundational elements of the Christian faith.

However, many hesitate to cut all ties with their church. They often wonder whether something is wrong with them. What led them on the road to doubt and prompted them to gradually disconnect? Many have most of their friends, and often quite a few of their relatives, in the church. They fear that leaving the church will cause havoc to their social life. Will it complicate their relationships with family members or mean losing lifelong friends, or worse? It is really worth taking the risk?

IS THIS BOOK FOR YOU?

I am a Seventh-day Adventist Seventh-day Adventist church member and a life-long pastor. I want to be upfront. I want this book to be positive. It always hurts me to see people around me leave my church. Surely, I am myself also deeply concerned about some trends that I see in my church. But, as a fellow-believer and as a pastor, and as someone who has dedicated his life to serving the church, I want to do what I can to help others who struggle with doubt and uncertainty.

The issues the Adventist Church is struggling with, and the challenges many Adventist men and women are facing, are not unique to Adventists. In some form or another they are also widespread in other Christian communities, but in this book I am primarily addressing people in the Adventist community. Yet I am not targeting all of them. My aim is not to provide support for those who are firmly anchored in the church. I hope this group will read some of the other things I write from time to time, and feel strengthened in their faith commitment when I happen to preach in their church. However, this book is not really for them, even though I hope many will obtain it, if only perhaps to give it to someone else whom they feel might benefit from reading it.

This book is also not primarily meant for those who left the church long ago and no longer have any use for the church—the Adventist Church or any other denomination—in their lives. Of course, if some in this category do read it and find something worthwhile in it, so much the better. But it is not primarily written with them in mind. I am specifically addressing those who are uncertain whether they want to stay or leave; for those who doubt whether the church still has something to offer them; for those who have serious doubts about important aspects of the faith they grew up with and once accepted as 'truth'; for those who have grave difficulty in accepting certain trends in the church; and for all those who feel they may no longer be able to see the church as their true spiritual home.

I do not profess to have the answers to all the questions the people in this category may have. I have no instant remedies for clearing all doubts and dissolving all uncertainties; I cannot and will not defend all decisions, projects and plans of the church. Sometimes I have myself been tempted to move towards the backdoor of the church. I disagree with some aspects of the traditional Adventist theology, and I refuse to read the Bible in the literal (and often fundamentalist) manner that seems so popular these days. Therefore, I am not providing a manual with easy answers that will tell you how to get rid of all your doubts and that will restore in a few moments your trust in the church as an organization and your confidence in all those who lead it and function in it.

Let me repeat it: I will try to be totally honest with myself and with you, the reader. I hope that reading this book will be a meaningful and rewarding experience for you. *I, for one, want to stay with my church.* And, even more importantly, *I do not want to lose my faith.*

As I was considering whether to write this book, someone told me about a small book that recently appeared in Australia. I bought a copy in the Adventist Book Center in Melbourne when I was visiting there. I read it with great interest, the more so since it echoed many of my own thoughts and feelings. It is entitled *Why I Try to Believe,* and is written by Nathan Brown, the leader of the Adventist publishing house in Australia.[12] I enjoyed having lunch with the author a week or so after I read his book, and comparing notes regarding our respective spiritual journeys.

Ryan Bell, a former minister of the Adventist Church in Hollywood (USA), who decided to live as an atheist for a year, wrote the preface for Nathan Brown's book. He did not know where his atheism-project might lead him or how it might change him. It was obviously not something he thought of one day and then implemented the next day. I know only snippets of Bell's personal history, from remarks made by people who know him and by following him on *Facebook*, but I suspect that his decision came as the climax of a long and excruciating process. By now a few years have passed since Bell began his experiment. He often writes about his experience and gives talks about it. It is clear that he did not end his experiment with atheism after twelve months. As far as I have been able to ascertain from a distance, it seems that he has continued to live as an atheist since he began his experimental year.

Nathan Brown and Ryan Bell have been friends for many years. Nathan acknowledges that he has many doubts, but he has very intentionally chosen another route than his friend Ryan. He does not want to abandon his faith, but wants to try to believe, in spite of his many doubts and uncertainties, and he hopes that his openness and honesty will stimulate his readers to give faith a new chance in their life. I have personally benefited from reading his book. I write from a different angle, but I share the same hope.

I do not know what my book will do for those who read it. Will it help at least some to persevere in their attempts to believe? Can we explore together some ways to live creatively and hopefully with our doubts and questions? Will it help at least a few readers to relate in a new and meaningful way to their church, in spite of moments when some of the things that happen seem totally irrelevant or even wrong? Will it convince at least some that God should still matter to them, that reading his Word can still inspire them and that faith—however feeble and wavering at times—can bring peace to their souls? I hope it will. If it does, I will feel greatly rewarded. Moreover, I expect that this project will also be good for my own soul! For I myself am as much the target for this book as the people I have just described.

1 www.reinderbruinsma.com
2 http://www.thetablet.co.uk/news/170/0/1-000-catholic-churches-in-holland-to-close-by-2025-pope-warned.
3 http://www.huffingtonpost.com/2014/11/05/catholic-church-new-york-closing_n_6097300.html.
4 Mark A. Knoll, *Turning Points: Decisive Moments in the History of Christianity* (Grand Rapids, MI: Baker Academic, 1997), p. 299.
5 Dean Kelly, *Why Conservative Churches Are Still Growing* (New York: Harper and Row, 1972), pp. 95, 96.
6 See the chapter 'Why "Mainline" Denominations Decline' in: Roger Finke and Rodney Stark: *The Churching of America 1776-1990: Winners and Losers in our Religious Economy* (New Brunswick, NJ: Rutgers University Press, 1992), pp. 237-275.
7 For a persuasive and intriguing treatment of the 'image problem' of Christianity with the current younger generations, see David Kinnaman and Gabe Lyons, *Un-Christian: What a New Generation Really Thinks about Christianity* (Grand Rapids, MI: Baker Books, 2007), and Dan Kimball, *They Like Jesus but not the Church: Insights from Emerging Generations* (Grand Rapids, MI: Zondervan, 2007).
8 http://edition.cnn.com/2015/05/12/living/pew-religion-study/
9 The *Barna group* is a prestigious research organization in the United States that focuses on issues regarding the relationship between faith and culture.
10 http://www.gotquestions.org/falling-away.html.
11 https://news.adventist.org/en/all-news/news/go/2015-10-13/church-accounts-for-lost-members/.
12 Nathan Brown, *Why I Try to Believe: An Experiment in Faith, Life and Stubborn Hope* (Warburton, Australia: Signs Publishing, 2015).

PART 1

Questions, uncertainties, doubts

CHAPTER 2

Christianity in crisis

SETTING THE STAGE

During part of my childhood years our family lived in a village some 20 miles (35 kilometers) north of Amsterdam. The population of just below 1,000 people was one hundred percent Caucasian. As far as I know all the villagers had Dutch nationality. Most people would have classified themselves as religious. Those who did not belong to any church were an exception and did not really fit into the social fabric. The village was about sixty percent Protestant and about forty percent Roman Catholic. The Catholics tended to live in one part of the village. The Protestants were split between two denominations: the Dutch Reformed Church and the Christian Reformed Church. The only anomalies were an elderly lady who had become a Jehovah's Witness, and our family. We were Seventh-day Adventists. People knew we were Protestants of some kind, more or less like Christian Reformed people, but who for some strange reason were going to church, somewhere in a nearby town, on Saturdays rather than on Sundays. Like many smaller places in the Netherlands, our village was characterized by a major degree of religious segregation. Protestant children did not play with Catholic boys and girls. Catholics tended to give their business to shops owned by co-religionists. And so on.

I realize that larger towns and cities in my native country of the Netherlands displayed a somewhat different pattern, but by and large in those not so long-gone days—'when I was young'—social life was a lot simpler and much more transparent than it is today. For one thing, society was much more homogeneous. People of foreign descent were few and far between. My country was Christian, apart from a few Jewish believers who had survived World War II and a small group of 'unbelievers.' Mosques and Hindu temples were virtually unknown and dark-skinned people were an exception. About one-third of the Dutch people were Catholics; most others belonged to half a dozen or so major Protestant denominations.

That was just half a century ago. In the meantime the picture has changed dramatically. After repeated influxes of large numbers of immigrants, the Netherlands has become an extremely diverse nation. Now, in the second decade of the twenty-first century, a full nineteen percent of the circa seventeen million Dutch people are of non-European origin, while many of the 'Europeans' may have Spanish, Portuguese, Greek, Hungarian or other origins. While thirty-one percent of the people continue to profess adherence to the Roman Catholic Church, only twenty-one percent now consider themselves Protestants—though their church involvement is often quite nominal. Today one in every twenty-five persons in the Netherlands is a Muslim, and a similar percentage belongs to other non-Christian faiths. Forty percent of the population no longer feels attached to any faith community at all.

This is the picture for the country as a whole.[1] The situation in some of the larger cities is, however, far more dramatic. Take Rotterdam for example, where you may find over 175 different nationalities. Only forty-eight percent of today's inhabitants of Rotterdam were born in the Netherlands. The statistics for Amsterdam are quite similar.

Besides the ethnic and cultural mixture, *religious* diversity has also become an irreversible fact of twenty-first century life. Only seventeen percent of the population of the Dutch capital regard themselves as Christians. With a fourteen percent share of the population, the Muslim faith is now the second largest religion in Amsterdam and is expected soon to be the largest. Besides mosques and a few synagogues, the city now has Buddhist temples and houses of worship for a range of other non-Christian religions. At the same time, many of the indigenous inhabitants indicate that they have no religious affiliation at all.[2] Yet secularism has not won the day in some parts of the city. When in the 1960s and 1970s the Bijlmer suburb, in the southeast of Amsterdam, was designed and built, no building plots were reserved for religious buildings. The authorities believed these would no longer be needed. Today, this has proven to be a serious miscalculation and it presents a major problem, as this area of the city now happens to be the most religious part of the country, after consecutive waves of immigrants, especially from the Caribbean region and parts of Africa, have brought a great variety of religious expressions with them!

THE WESTERN WORLD HAS CHANGED

What has happened in the Netherlands has also occurred in many other parts of the Western world. The major cities of Western Europe, the United States, Canada and Australia have become totally cosmopolitan. Whereas in 1970 18.2 percent of New Yorkers were foreign-born, this percentage has risen to over thirty-seven percent by 2014.[3] A similar development may be seen, for example, in Toronto (Canada). According to the 2011 *National Household Survey,* published by *Statistics Canada,* 48.6 percent of Toronto's inhabitants are foreign-born—which makes it one of the most diverse cities in the world.[4] Of Melbourne's (Australia) 4.3 million citizens over thirty-eight percent are foreign born. A little bit of *googling* will reveal similar figures for many major US cities, and for European cities such as Paris, London and Brussels, and many other population centers. For countries as a whole the figures are lower, but nonetheless very significant, and on the rise. In 2014 over fourteen percent of the people living in the United Kingdom were foreign-born—half of these, or about three million people, living in London. One in every four Australians was born elsewhere, while for the USA the figure is almost fourteen percent.[5]

Religious diversity in the Western world has increased even more sharply. Although in the last few centuries Christians have been active in spreading the message of Christ 'to the ends of the earth,' and hundreds of millions of people have accepted Christ as a result—both in the Western world and elsewhere—the percentage of Christians in the total world population has not noticeably increased. Reliable statistics indicate that in 1900 about one third of all people on our planet considered themselves Christians. At the beginning of the present century this was still the case.[6]

But though the global percentage of Christians has remained stable during the last few generations, Christianity has lost significant strength in the Western World—today also often referred to as the *North,* in contrast with the so-called developing world, which is now labelled as the *South.* One of the important developments in recent Christian history has been the shift of the Christian presence and influence from the North to the South. According to Philip Jenkins, an authority on trends in the contemporary religious world, the move of Christianity from the North to the South is a truly global phenomenon.[7] In spite of a substantial population growth, the total number of Christians in the North changed only marginally between 1910 and 2010—from 502 million to 509 million. This is in contrast with Christianity in the South. The best estimate for the number of Christians in the South in 1910 was 856 million, while a century later the number had risen to 1.3 billion.

Roman Catholic experts estimate that in 2025 the total number of Catholics in North America and Europe will be almost at the same level as it was in 2000. However, in Africa the number of Catholics is expected to have grown in that 25-year period from 120 million to 228 million, in Latin America from 461 million to 606 million and in Asia from 110 million to 160 million!

Similar patterns are clearly present in Seventh-day Adventism. Since 1980 membership in North America has doubled, whereas in Europe it has increased by about thirty percent—much of this growth being related to immigration. But note that in the same period the membership in Inter-America grew from 646,000 to more than 3.5 million. An astonishing rate of growth was also seen in South America and Africa, where the 2015 membership was over five and over ten times, respectively, of what it was in 1980.[8]

Perhaps even more significant than the statistics regarding the number of Christians in the North are the data about average church attendance. It is incredibly difficult to arrive at reliable figures. Many denominations are very reluctant to share this kind of information, while many church members tend to overstate the number of times they actually go to church. But the figures that can be found are quite alarming. A few examples must suffice, but they illustrate what is happening. With about 2.5 percent of the population attending church more or less regularly, Denmark has the lowest percentage of churchgoers in Europe, but the other Scandinavian countries show percentages that are not much higher.[9] In Poland—one of Europe's most religious countries—the number of people regularly attending mass has dropped from fifty-three percent in 1987 to less than forty percent at present.[10] Even though recent waves of immigrants have somewhat boosted church attendance figures in the United Kingdom, most reports on church attendance show only single digit figures. While some polls in the USA report that about forty percent of all Americans still regularly attend church, other reports indicate that the percentage is probably less than half that number.[11] A far lower percentage applies to Australia. At the same time the number of people in the Western world who openly state they are atheists or agnostics is growing rapidly. *Gallup International* conducted a survey in 2012 and found that in fifty-seven countries no less than thirteen percent of the respondents said they were 'convinced atheists.' A similar percentage emerged from a poll in sixty-five countries in 2015.[12]

THE MOST FUNDAMENTAL CHANGE

The world in which we live has changed dramatically in another, even more fundamental, way. Without exaggeration it can be said that the world—the Western world in particular—has moved into a new era. Or to use the terms that have become part of today's lingo: *modernity* has given way to *postmodernity.*

There is no shortage of books that list the main characteristics of the postmodern man and woman. Those interested in pursuing this in more depth should read up on the topic.[13] Here I will just summarize some of the most noticeable aspects of the postmodern approach to life.

1. For a long period of time people believed in *continuous progress.* Science would help us make life better and better. This idea of progress is now largely a thing of the past. The world is simply facing too many problems and science does not always seem to be the unmitigated blessing it was once thought to be.
2. Scientists are now more modest in their claims than in the past. They confess that they often tend to see what they want to see, and that many of the so-called *foundations of science* may not be so certain after all.
3. Past generations believed in *absolutes.* Things were either right or wrong. People were looking for the *Truth.* Today, for most people there are no such absolutes. They claim to have their own private *truths.* Communities and cultures have their own 'language games' and their own ways of operating. Everything is subjective, relative, uncertain, preliminary, and ambiguous.
4. If there is not one absolute Truth, on what basis can Christians then claim that their religion has more 'truth' than, for example, Islam or Rastafarianism? Why is the Bible to be preferred above the Book of Mormon or the Koran?
5. The *grand stories* (so-called 'metanarratives') and the grand ideals of the past—such as socialism, communism, capitalism, and also Christianity—have lost their power. We no longer have 'stories' that may serve as a framework for everything we say and do. We must be content with more limited, partial explanations that need constant revision.
6. Postmodern people like *combining incompatible elements.* In architecture and in the arts we find a great interest in collation, a mixing of artistic styles, a blurring of the lines between real life and fiction, between the real and the virtual.
7. People realize more and more that they live in a *global village.* The computer—the symbol of postmodernity *par excellence*— gives them instant access to the world. Yet, at the same time, *global* strategies and alliances are under suspicion, and there is a growing interest in regional and *local* issues.
8. Perhaps most importantly in the context of what we are going to discuss in this book is the fact that the postmodern person has a strong dislike for *religious institutions* with their hierarchical

power structures, inflexible creeds and doctrines that are set in concrete and must be adhered to.

9. Related to this reluctance to get involved with an organization—religious or otherwise—is a hesitancy to enter into deep, long lasting *commitments*. This impacts strongly on the viability of clubs and associations, but also on personal relationships and sustained church activities.

10. Postmodern believers want to *pick and choose*. They embrace the things they agree with, but discard doctrines and religious traditions that do not, or no longer, appeal to them.

11. Yet the postmodern person is *open to spirituality*. Mystery is OK. A non-rational, New Age-type approach to the questions of life is popular. The emphasis has shifted from religious *truth* that is codified in doctrine to personal *experience*.

Once you are aware of the main characteristics of the postmodern mindset, you see the impact of postmodern thinking everywhere. Look at some recent buildings in Western cities: no longer the 'modern' box-like, monotonous structures of concrete, steel and glass. Ornamentation is back and styles from different periods are combined, so that postmodern buildings can 'tell their own story' rather than the standard 'modern' story of power, order and efficiency. You will also easily detect postmodern trends in many recent novels, which blend stories from different periods and/or mix real life situations with the world of fantasy. And you notice it in films that leave you wondering where history ends and fiction begins. You find the ambiguity in the political arena, as for instance in parts of Europe, where a majority of the people support some form of European unity, but at the same time will do almost anything to protect their national sovereignty and local culture (and often their local dialect).

One quickly detects the postmodern approach of many 'Western' people to religion and to the church. Absolute statements about truth are largely replaced by 'what works for me,' and many Bible scholars claim there are as many legitimate ways to interpret the Bible as there are readers. *In the Western world Christianity has become just one religious option among a series of world religions—all are considered* equally valid, but historically and culturally conditioned responses of the human self to the mysterious Beyond!

A BIT OF HISTORY

It is important to understand what kind of world we live in today, and what society we are part of in this day and age, but it is also essential to know a bit of history. John Michael Crichton (1942-2008), an American author of science fiction books and a producer of films and television programs, quoted a Professor Johnston (a character in his book *Timeline*) as saying, 'If you don't know history, you don't know anything. You are a leaf that does not know it was part of a tree.'[14] This truism applies to all spheres of life, and certainly also to the domain of religion and church. Talking sensibly about religious matters and about current trends in religious life and in the church is only possible if we can put things into some historical framework. To understand what is happening in today's church is impossible without knowing something about its history, its past experiences and its ups and downs. Getting a grip on what is happening in our day and age in the religious world (as we briefly explored in chapter one) and understanding something of the new ways in which religion is practiced and experienced by vast numbers of people in the Western world of the twenty-first century, requires at least a little knowledge of church history.

For Seventh-day Adventists, to understand the present trends in their church, and the way many church members react to these developments, also presupposes an awareness of how their denomination fits into the greater religious scene of Christianity, and, in particular, into Protestantism. Dealing with the issues that will figure prominently in this book demands some knowledge of the origin and developments of Adventism, but also of the past of Christianity and of the background of the general religious climate in today's postmodern world.

A MIXED BAG

The history of Christianity presents us with a very mixed bag of phenomena and events. The New Testament pictures the young church as a vibrant community that spread in just a few decades to many parts of the Middle East and of Europe, and even further, to Asia and Africa. This phenomenal church growth did not take place without problems or challenges. And though Paul's words must be understood as a literary exaggeration, they do indicate that something extraordinary took place. He writes to the church in Colosse that the gospel had now been proclaimed 'to every creature under heaven' (Colossians 1:21).

In the next few centuries the strong growth of the church continued. Christian theology developed—partly because of the many strange ideas that surfaced and needed to be straightened out, and because of the numerous questions that needed answers. The writers of early second and third century Christian documents, and the so-called 'church fathers' of the centuries that followed, gave structure to the church's theology and organization. It was agreed which writings were to be accepted as 'inspired' Scripture. The basic Christian doctrines, about the nature of God and the mystery of the Trinity, and about the way in which the divinity and humanity of Christ were united in one unique Person; about the personhood of the Holy Spirit and about the basis of our salvation, were hammered out. Strong leaders emerged in various places, and a few Christian centers—Rome prominently among them—steadily gained in prestige and authority.

The church entered a new phase in its history when, in the fourth century, the Roman emperor Constantine decided to give Christianity a privileged status in his empire. The future would prove this to be a dubious blessing. It allowed the church to expand further without fearing periods of persecutions that had earlier cost so many lives and caused so much hardship. But it also increasingly tied the church to worldly politics with all its negative consequences.

Over time the medieval church developed, with the bishop of Rome in a prominent position, leading to the growth of the papacy as the most prestigious center of authority. In many places the purity of the gospel of Christ was diluted into a sorry mixture of authentic faith and pagan superstition. As 'heathen' peoples were converted, often by external force rather than by inner conviction, many unchristian ideas and practices entered the church. At the same time theologians were often unduly influenced by the writings of non-Christian philosophers of the classical era—the influence of which can be detected even in quite a bit of today's theology. Church leaders were often more concerned about acquiring power and wealth, and in fighting their battles for more political influence, than in providing good pastoral care and solid religious instruction for the people entrusted to their care. Immorality and political intrigue frequently obscured or replaced the desire to be a true disciple of Christ.

In time this sad state of affairs inspired the rise of various reform movements, led by such courageous men as John Wycliffe and Jan Hus (also often referred to as John Huss), and eventually to the 'reformation' of the church in the sixteenth century. This reformation not only brought a rediscovery of the glorious fact that we are saved by grace rather than by our own works, or by the intervention of a sacerdotal clergy or even the payment of money. It also gave the Bible back to the common people and protested (hence the name *Protestants*) against many abuses and incorrect teachings that had crept into the church. Some reformers were more radical than others, and in retrospect it must be acknowledged that many aspects that also badly needed reform were downplayed or ignored. And in the centuries that followed it was often not sufficiently realized that the church must always continue on the path of a further restoration of the teachings of Christ. As Martin Luther stated, the church is *semper reformanda*—always in need of further reform.

Although the 'church of Rome' also realized that changes were needed, and some changes were indeed effected during the so-called Counter-Reformation, the deep rift between Catholicism and Protestantism became a decisive reality in Christianity—after an earlier schism (1054) had already caused a permanent divide between the 'orthodox' churches of the East and the church of the West.

Roman Catholicism was quite successful in keeping its many varieties of experience and establishments, as for instance its broad range of monastic orders, under its ecclesiastical umbrella. The Church of

Rome saw periods of strength but also times of decline and relative weakness. Tragically, from its beginning, the Protestant world never showed a united front. Lutheranism and Calvinism developed along different paths, and the fragmentation of Protestant Christianity into numerous 'denominations' has continued ever since, in spite of some successes at reunification that resulted from ecumenical endeavors.

In spite of all their theological differences and their wide diversity in governance and practice, the many different Protestant denominations may be classified as belonging to a few main streams: the traditional 'conservative' churches, the traditional more 'liberal' churches, evangelicalism and, more recently, a rapidly expanding Pentecostalism. Periods of decline and of spiritual lethargy tended to be followed by waves of revivalism and bursts of missionary activity. These characterized much of the developments in nineteenth-century Protestantism. Adventism came out of one of the main revival movement in the United States in the mid-nineteenth century. The activities of William Miller (1782-1849) were an important part of the final phase of the Second Great Revival of American Christianity. As the Seventh-day Adventist church outgrew its Millerite origins, it never lost its American character and still shows many traces of the milieu in which it originated and developed.

In the twentieth century and in the early years of the twenty-first century, Christianity continues to inspire millions of people around the globe. Organized Christianity still offers a fascinating array of ideas, activities and services. Mission is still a very major enterprise, as statistics about the numbers of missionary organizations, their budgets and the numbers of missionary personnel show. But Christianity must increasingly compete with other religious and non-religious worldviews—even in those territories where it long used to have its undisputed power base. A rapid and thorough process of secularization, and the emergence of a subtle—and at times not so subtle—postmodern culture, is proving to be extremely challenging to the Christian faith and to ecclesiastical organizations and institutions. And all this has affected Adventism in more ways than many of its leaders, as well as adherents in the pews, realize.

This brief sketch of a history of twenty centuries is, of course, not only very superficial and incomplete, but it also fails to do justice to the many phenomena, ideas and personalities that were part of this history. The stories about the darkest periods of the Christian past, the scandals of the Borgias, the annals of the Inquisition, the abuses of simony[15] and indulgences, certainly do not give us a full and accurate picture. Even in the bleakest periods women and men lived and worked in and for the church with great piety and at enormous personal sacrifice. Beautiful works of art were created and inspiring spiritual books were written. We are indebted to the works of astute and brilliant theologians of all ages. We find inspiring role models in the lives of many of the mystics, spiritual innovators and social activists of the past. People like Augustine, Anselm, Abelard, St Francis of Assisi, Hildegard von Bingen, John Wesley, Jonathan Edwards, and many others, stand out as genuine followers of Christ, even though some of their theological views and methods may have been inadequate. On the other hand, some ideas and actions of Protestant heroes, such as Martin Luther and John Calvin, were totally appalling. Luther's role in some of the political clashes of his days is most deplorable and his anti-Semitism is something most Protestants today find abhorrent. John Calvin is not only known for his valuable theological contribution in his Christian Institutes, but also for his role in the execution of Michael Servetus, who disagreed with him in his theology. This pattern of great courage and spiritual insight, in combination with significant lapses of judgment and theological errors, has characterized most leaders of the past—even those who have made notable contributions to the cause of Christianity.

In the next chapter we will move away from the church in general and focus on the current state of Adventism. Not all is well, and I believe we may indeed speak of a crisis. While there are many good things and many elements that we must protect and keep for the future, there are also things that many Adventist church members, with good reason, want to distance themselves from. I count myself among them. And for the many who are 'on the margins' of the church the question is whether the good still outweighs the things they find problematic or worse.

1   http://www.amsterdam.info/netherlands/population/.
2   http://www.iamsterdam.com/en/local/about-amsterdam/people-culture/
    religion-spirituality.
3   http://www.nyc.gov/html/dcp/pdf/census/nny2013/chapter2.pdf.
4   https://en.wikipedia.org/wiki/Demographics_of_Toronto.
5   http://www.usatoday.com/story/news/2015/09/28/us-foreign-born-
    population-nears-high/72814674/.
6   A few specialized agencies collect such statistics. A good, annually updated
    source is the *International Bulletin of Missionary Research.*
7   Philip Jenkins, *The Next Christendom: The Coming of Global Christianity* (New
    York: Oxford University Press, 2011).
8   Office of Archive and Statistics: https://www.adventistarchives.org for the annual
    statistical reports from which these data have been drawn.
9   https://viaintegra.wordpress.com/european-church-attendance/.
10 http://worldnews.nbcnews.com/_news/2013/03/05/17184588.
11 http://www.churchleaders.com/pastors/pastor-articles/139575-7-startling-
    facts-an-up-close-look-at-church-attendance-in-america.html.
12 https://en.wikipedia.org/wiki/Demographics_of_atheism.
13 See e.g. my e-book that may be downloaded from Amazon.com: *Present Truth
    Revisited: An Adventist Perspective on Postmodernism,* 2014.
14 http://www.brainyquote.com/quotes/topics/topic_history.html#GxsDIcsLv
    CTD3HqI.99.
15 Simony occurs when people are able to buy a church office for themselves or for
    a relative. The word originates from the story in Acts 8.

CHAPTER 3

Recent trends in Adventism

Most Seventh-day Adventists who have studied the history of their movement gratefully acknowledge the many wonderful and inspiring things in the past. They have indeed plenty of reason to marvel about the growth of the Adventist Church, from a handful of disappointed men and women in a rural area of Northeastern America—who were deluded into expecting the return of Jesus Christ in 1844—into a church of over 19 million baptized members, with a presence in over 200 countries. But the annals of Adventist history also contain dark pages and do not present a consistent picture of wise decisions, theological acumen, true sacrifice and genuine commitment. We have experienced ugly doctrinal fights, and at times seen blatant power struggles. The church has been successful, but from time to time major initiatives had to be aborted, while not all institutions flourished or survived.

Below we will look at some of these things in greater detail. But let me at this point make it clear that, when I say some negative things about Christianity in general, it is not because I have given up on the Christian faith and no longer subscribe to its values. And when I criticize my own church, it is not because I have an ax to grind, or because I have been treated badly by my employing church organizations and am looking for a chance of taking revenge. My church is dear to me and I have great respect for many of its leaders—past and present. Most of my social network is in the church. I have been a church employee for all of my working life, and by and large the church has been good to me. I had many interesting and satisfying assignments and had the opportunity to travel to over eighty countries. As a retiree I still enjoy the regular invitations for teaching appointments, and I still love to preach.

All of this does not, however, mean that I am happy with everything that happens in my church, and that I fully agree with all the things it officially says. In fact, I am extremely worried about a number of developments and have serious questions about some of the official beliefs I am supposed to subscribe to. Nor does it mean that I am blind to the struggles of many of the people I meet as I visit churches in my country, and talk to numerous members, and as I read the e-mails and the responses to things I have written in articles and books and in my weekly blogs—from people all over the world, but especially from fellow-believers in Western Europe and the United States. Therefore, I will have to discuss these issues of concern at some length in the pages that follow. I do this because I love my church and I truly care for the people who doubt and struggle and, in many cases, are 'believers on the margins'—who are at the edges of the church—uncertain whether or not they want to stay.

I believe that the present crisis in Adventism cannot be properly understood if it is looked at in isolation from the crisis in many Christian churches in the Western world and from what has been happening to religion and faith in recent decades. And when I refer to the past of the Christian church in general, and to that of the Seventh-day Adventist Church in particular, it is because I am absolutely convinced that we must learn from past experiences. These, I believe, may strengthen our confidence that ultimately, somehow, things will work out well. Events and personalities of the past have inspired many and helped them find the courage to continue in the present. But there have also been mistakes, unfortunate decisions and regrettable statements that may serve as painful lessons for the present and for the future. Seeing these will give us, hopefully, the determination to work for change and to look at our faith with greater depth. George Santayana (1863-1952), an American philosopher, once said, 'Those who do not remember the past are condemned to repeat it.'

THE STRENGTH OF ADVENTISM

Today the Christian church in the Western world is facing a deep crisis. In the previous chapters I have mentioned some of the immense challenges the church is encountering. At present the church is not simply going through a period of decline—as it has from time to time done in the past—but its very survival in the secularized, postmodern world of Europe, the United States, and other parts of the Western world, is at stake. The biblical scenario of the reduction of God's people to a small 'remnant' has now become a very distinct possibility or even probability. I repeat what I have already said: whether it wants it or not, and whether it realizes it or not, the Adventist Church in 'the North' is a part of Western Christianity. It may be unique in some ways, but it shares the same secular context with other Christians. Its internal and external publics are mostly postmodern—or *post*-postmodern, as some would say—and react to Adventism in the same way as the majority of the people react to any form of institutional Christianity.

During my teenage years (and for quite some time beyond them), the members of the Adventist Church in the Netherlands were urged to participate in an annual campaign to solicit money for Adventist missions. Government regulations did not allow us to ask people directly for a donation. We had to sell a specially prepared magazine for a set price. Of course, if people wanted to pay more for the magazine, we would not deter them from doing so, but selling magazines was the basis for our so-called 'harvest ingathering' campaign. Most years I would participate and do my share, be it with limited enthusiasm. Later, when I was in my late thirties and early forties, I actually served as the editor of this annual publication. I must admit that by that time I relied on others to go from door to door in order to sell my editorial product!

I mention this because one of the most important features of the magazine was the page with a statistical report that applauded the accomplishment of Adventist Missions. Adventists were working in so many countries in the world, publishing books in so many hundreds of languages and preaching the gospel over so many radio stations.

Special attention was called to the vast network of thousands of Adventist schools for primary, secondary and higher education, and to the hundreds of hospitals, clinics and dispensaries around the world. Those who went selling the magazine never failed to point the person at the door to these wonderful statistics and then underlined that by purchasing the magazine the buyer would support this magnificent effort to serve humanity.

When I was in my teenage years the Adventist Church had just passed the one million member mark. Though Adventism of the 1950s and 1960s was much smaller than it is today, I nonetheless felt a certain pride in being part of this vast worldwide organization. And even today, as I travel, it always gives me a thrill when I suddenly discover the name Seventh-day Adventist on the facade of a building. In some countries the chances of seeing this are quite small, but in others the name is displayed quite prominently in many places. The sense of belonging to something big still makes me feel good, and I know that I share this sentiment with many of my Adventist colleagues and friends.

But there was not only a sense of pride. In the not so distant past in many Western countries Adventism was often seen as a foreign (i.e. American) sect. Leaders of other denominations frequently wondered openly whether Adventists were in fact real Christians. Unfortunately, if people knew something about Adventists, it was often only about the things that Adventists were 'forbidden' to do. Our public profile was extremely poor: we were best known for what we did *not* do, rather than for the ideals we had embraced. There were positive exceptions. While traveling abroad some people were cared for in an Adventist hospital and gained a favorable impression of Adventism, and some had worked with an Adventist colleague who had lived his faith in a positive way.

Years ago, when our family moved to a new town, my wife told our next door neighbor that we were Seventh-day Adventists. 'Oh no, not again,' she exclaimed. She had lived in Canada next to an Adventist family, who for years had incessantly tried to 'convert' her, and she did not want a repeat of that situation. Fortunately, over time my wife developed a good relationship with this neighbor. When we moved to our current address our next-door neighbors fortunately reacted quite differently. They had lived in Switzerland with Adventist neighbors who had been very pleasant and for whom they had nothing but praise.

The reputation of our church in the micro-cosmos in which we live depends very much on how we model our faith, and on our social skills in interacting with people of other faiths or no faith at all. But in the wider society things are different. It has been an uphill battle in many countries for the Adventist Church to gain a positive reputation. Gradually our public profile has somewhat improved. Many church leaders and theologians have become convinced that, in spite of some peculiarities, Adventists are after all *bona fide* Protestant Christians and can be accepted and relied upon as partners in interchurch activities. As more and more Adventists have gained respect in their professional roles, and have told others in a positive manner about their commitment to the Adventist faith and faith community, Adventism has become less strange and objectionable in the eyes of many. I have personally had the pleasure of interacting with many representatives of other denominations and with theologians of different backgrounds in the world of academia. As the years have gone by my religious persuasion usually ceased to be a barrier. The fact that in many countries the Adventist Church—in spite of the fierce objections of a hard core of conservative members against any ties with other Christians—has entered into some kind of relationship with national councils of churches or similar associations has also helped to remove a lot of suspicion and reluctance towards us.

Nowadays most Adventist pastors are considerably better educated than their colleagues were a generation or so ago, and many have also studied at non-Adventist universities. It has not only helped them to become professionals in their work but has also given them more self-confidence in relating to their congregation(s) and in their interaction with colleagues and public officials. I have found that my credibility as a pastor and as an author and church administrator was often at critical moments positively affected by the fact that I have a final degree from a reputable British university. It has helped me in crucial circumstances to be accepted on equal terms with my peers of other faiths and other professionals. A number of Adventist colleges where our pastors are educated have evolved from non-accredited Bible schools to institutions with university status, fully recognized by the relevant accrediting organizations. This also has been a factor in the growing respectability of the Adventist Church in our society.

THE ENVY OF MANY OTHERS

It is no overstatement to say that the Adventist Church has developed an amazingly strong organization. Its organizational strength is not just visible in its four-tiered structure of (1) General Conference/divisions; (2) unions; (3) conferences; and (4) local churches. Detailed policies have been developed for the smooth operation of the ecclesiastical machinery, with clear election procedures for choosing leaders; with detailed rules for the functioning of the various church units; and with carefully defined rights and privileges of the constituencies at the various levels. Leaders of other denominations have often expressed their admiration—or even their envy—for the way the Adventist Church is organized.

Although any denomination can always use more money—and usually never ceases to appeal for greater generosity on the part of its members—the Adventist organization has a solid financial basis. Worldwide annual church income now stands at over 3.3 billon US dollars. This includes tithes and offerings, but not the much bigger figure of the financial operation of the institutions of the church.[1]

The Adventist Church has remained remarkably united, while Protestantism in general has become terribly fragmented. No one knows exactly how many Christian denominations exist in the world. Many of these are very small, but some churches (for instance in Africa) that are unknown to most of us have millions of members. One source reports that the United States is currently home to over 1,500 religious organizations and that worldwide every day three new religions are born.[2] American Protestantism has experienced a greater proliferation than is perhaps seen anywhere else. If you want a good overview of the American religious scene, find a recent edition of the *Handbook of Denominations in the United States* (by Frank S. Mead), which provides a useful description of over 200 major religious bodies in the USA.[3]

Over the years some groups have left the Adventist Church and formed their own movements. There also were dissidents who had sympathizers, and who wrote books, but did not organize a separate movement. Some prominent examples were J.H. Kellogg, Dudley M. Canright, Ludwig R. Conradi, A.T. Jones, E.J. Waggoner and A.F. Ballenger. Some small movements that were (more or less) organized included: the 'Holy Flesh' Movement, the Shepherd's Rod Movement, the notorious Branch Davidians, and groups around Robert Brinsmead.[4] The most important split occurred when the Seventh-day Adventist Reform Movement separated from the main Adventist body as the result of controversies about participating in World War I. This group organized itself as an independent denomination that currently has some 40,000 members in over 130 countries. In addition to this tragic secession some other small groups have turned their backs on the Adventist Church. But looking back it is truly amazing to see how strongly Adventism has remained united. Compare this, for instance, with the Baptist movement. The Baptist World Alliance reports that it comprises 228 different Baptist organizations.[5] And not all Baptist denominations are members of the Alliance! Many of them have a separate national or regional organization, and represent a wide range of theological opinions, from somewhat liberal to extremely fundamentalist. Overall one may say that the Adventist Church has, indeed, stayed remarkably united.

DEVELOPING A MATURE THEOLOGY

Seventh-day Adventist theology has changed significantly over the years. Adventist historian George R. Knight once stated that James White, one of the church's founders, would not have recognized current Adventist beliefs as the doctrines of his denomination and might not even have wanted to be a member of today's Adventist Church.[6] The development of Adventist beliefs is a fascinating topic that we cannot deal with at any length in this book. A few remarks must suffice. It is important to emphasize that the full package of twenty-eight *Fundamental Beliefs* did not fall from heaven, early on in Adventist history. Contemporary Adventist theological thinking is the result of a long and gradual development. It started with people with a background in different Protestant movements, who had gone through a major disappointment when their expectation of Christ's return remained unfulfilled. Within a few years they arrived at a broad consensus with regard to a number of points—such as, for instance, the Sabbath and an explanation for the 1844 debacle. They developed a 'sanctuary' doctrine and acknowledged that 'the gift of prophecy' was manifested amongst them. Soon they also accepted the view of death as a 'sleep,' and denied that there is an immortal soul that goes to heaven immediately after death. After some time they also agreed that theirs was a worldwide mission: all people had to be warned about the end and had to be confronted with God's final message of impending judgment. But several other doctrines were crystallized only as the decades passed.

Much of Adventism in its early period was rather legalistic. An important meeting in 1888 addressed this issue, but legalism has remained a continuous challenge. Yet official church theology would from then onwards ever more strongly emphasize that salvation is not through human works but results solely from faith in Christ's sacrifice for humanity. In the twentieth century—and particularly from the 1960s onward—the basic Christian doctrines, such as those concerning the Trinity, the natures of Christ, the personhood of the Holy Spirit, and the atonement, received much more attention than before, when the focus had been almost exclusively on the uniquely Adventist doctrinal views. When discussing the growth and strength of Adventism it is important to remember this gradual maturing of Adventist theological thinking.

ADVENTISM IN CRISIS?

But not all is well in the Adventist Church. Far from it. Many feel that recent developments in Adventism indicate that today the unity of the church is in great danger. Is this indeed the case? Could it be that Adventism—in particular in the West—is doomed to shrink and ultimately disappear? If so, would this be mainly due to the general malaise in Western Christianity, or are there some specific reasons why Adventism (at least in parts of the Western world) may not survive? Let us not say too hastily that the Lord will prevent the demise of the Adventist Church. It has happened before that Christian churches have declined and then disappeared altogether.

It has often been suggested that Christian churches are social organizations that go through a predictable cycle. A well-known model is that of sociologist of religion David O. Moberg (b. 1922).[7] He suggested that religious organizations typically go through five consecutive stages. In the *first* stage the new organization is started because of dissatisfaction with existing situations. A few people get together. Some new insights emerge as these people meet and share their ideas and attract likeminded individuals. At this point the leadership is mostly informal and charismatic in nature. In the *second* stage the organization acquires a more defined organizational structure. The aims and ideas are clarified and a consensus is reached regarding norms and values. This stage is characterized by strong recruitment activities. Then, in the *third* stage, the growing organization reaches a state of maximum efficiency with many innovative activities. The leadership tends to become more rational, rather than mostly charismatic. The organization gradually becomes more centralized and receives recognition from society. Stage *four* is often marked by an increasing institutionalization, usually with a growing bureaucracy. Norms and values become less distinct, and members tend to become more and more passive. The *final* stage sees the onset of disintegration. The organization suffers from formalism, bureaucracy, or worse. The administrative structures no longer connect with the actual questions and needs of the community. The people lose confidence in their leaders and new fringe groups tend to form on the margins. This, in fact, spells the beginning of the end of the movement.

If there is some validity to this model—and I think there is—it raises the important question *in which stage does the Adventist Church in the Western world currently find itself.* A few might say that we are still at stage three. This may indeed be true for the church in parts of the South. But I suspect that most of those who live in the Western world, and have given the matter some careful thought, will agree that we are probably at stage four, or even already at stage five. If so, we do not necessarily have to understand this as an unconditional prophecy, or as our inescapable fate. But, at the very least, it is a stern warning that we are in a serious crisis and that some drastic changes are needed to turn the tide. I believe that what Anglican bishop John Shelby Spong once said of the Christian church in general—that it *must change or die*—most definitely also applies to Adventism in the Western world.[8]

UNEASINESS ABOUT THE INSTITUTIONAL CHURCH

When a decade or so from now Adventist historians look back at developments in their church, they may perhaps point to the General Conference in San Antonio (Texas, USA) in 2015 as the moment when some unfortunate trends became much more visible than they had ever been.[9] When asked how he had experienced these meetings, where some 2,500-plus delegates from all over the world had assembled to elect leaders and make decisions that affect the future of their church, one Adventist university teacher referred to a few major shifts he had noted. It was abundantly clear, he said, that the South had become more aware of its potential influence and was more willing than in the past to use its numerical strength to overrule the wishes of the North. He also pointed to some other developments. He saw a shift from a spiritual overtone to a more political atmosphere, and a theological move from the 'middle' towards the 'right.' It appeared to him that the discussions about changes in the *Church Manual* indicated that this important document is gradually becoming *prescriptive* of what must be followed, rather than *descriptive* of a common way of dealing with organizational matters in the local church. In addition, he felt that the extensive debate on changes in the *Fundamental Beliefs* manifested an increasingly creedal trend. Furthermore, he observed that the role of the president of the denomination was becoming more and more 'imperial.'[10] We will return to these various 'shifts' in later pages, but first we will look at the concerns of many regarding the way in which the church machinery tends to operate these days.

The organizational model of the Adventist Church is a mix of elements that have been inherited from different traditions. The insistence on the separation between church and state comes from the 'free-church' tradition that is rooted in the Radical Reformation, and was transplanted to the United States where it became the norm rather than the exception. Adventism adopted organizational elements from Calvinism, as well as from Lutheranism, while much was simply carried over from Methodism and from the Christian Connection[11] movement, to which some key leaders in the early Adventist movement had belonged. The terminology of 'conferences' and 'general conference' hails from the strong Methodist influence. At the same time the four-tiered structure of the church—GC/divisions, unions, conferences, and local churches—has taken on a distinctly hierarchical nature with a Roman Catholic flavor. And, whether we like it or not, the American political system also left its indelible mark on the way the Adventist Church is organized. It has given the church a presidential form of leadership (but unfortunately not with the same balance of powers that is built into the American political system).

To the European mind, the presidential system seems undesirable. No European head of state or prime minister (as e.g. in Germany, the United Kingdom or even France) has the same kind of broad executive power, and can change and determine the direction of the country in the same way an American president can. Likewise, in the church in Europe union and conference leaders are first and foremost team leaders. Presidents chair meetings, they propose initiatives, but they must always ensure they have the backing of their committees and be careful how they introduce their own initiatives. I have served as a union president in my country. I believe I had the trust and respect of most church workers and of most church members, but I was always keenly aware of the fact that my powers were limited, and I knew when to refrain from pushing my own ideas too strongly—however brilliant I sometimes thought they were.

It bothers me, and many with me in Europe, but also elsewhere in the Western world and perhaps even beyond that—and even in the USA— that presidents of church entities have inordinate power and can to a large extent determine the church's agenda for the period they are in office. This is particularly true for the way the president of the world church can influence the direction of the entire denomination. At this point a bit of history may again be useful, as it illustrates how recent General Conference presidents have put their stamp on the periods during which they held the presidency.

FIVE CHURCH PRESIDENTS

Reuben Figuhr (1893-1986) led the Adventist Church from 1954 to 1966. Adventist historians characterize the period of his presidency as one of stability and openness. Figuhr was much less concerned about the influence of 'modern' and 'liberal' tendencies than would be the case under his successor. Two major projects are proof of the willingness of the church to break theological new ground (or at least to allow for this): the preparation of the (ever since) controversial book *Seventh-day Adventists Answer Questions on Doctrine*[12] and the seven-volume *Seventh-day Adventist Bible Commentary*, edited by F.D. Nichol.[13]

Robert Pierson (1911-1989) was extremely concerned about the theological direction of the church and did all he could to turn the tide. A close look at his presidency (1966-1979) shows uncanny parallels with the present administration, in particular with regard to the 'revival and reformation' theme that was launched by Pierson and later resurrected by Wilson.[14]

The next Adventist world leader was *Neal C. Wilson* (1920-2010), the father of the current GC president. During his presidency (1979-1990) the church saw considerable expansion. In 1979 the worldwide membership stood at almost 3.4 million; it had grown to over 5.5 million by 1990. The *Global Mission* initiative was among Wilson's ambitious programs intended to strengthen the outreach of the denomination. During its General Conference session in Dallas (Texas, USA) in 1980 the church adopted the twenty-seven *Fundamental Beliefs*. These twenty-seven points[15] became the basis for the revised document that was approved in San Antonio. Many have characterized Neal C. Wilson as a politician; one of the victims of church politics in the Wilson era was Desmond Ford (b. 1929).[16]

To the great surprise of most delegates to the 1990 session in Indianapolis (Indiana, USA), the relatively unknown *Robert Folkenberg* (1941-2015) was elected president. Folkenberg will be remembered for his fascination with new technology, but also for his many initiatives to facilitate the further growth of the church. Theologically he was rather conservative and, like Pierson, concerned to halt liberalizing tendencies. A comprehensive document entitled *Total Commitment* was officially accepted by the church, shortly before Folkenberg was forced to resign from office. Its intention was to make compliance with the content of this document a prerequisite for leadership and teaching assignments. The document found its way into the *SDA Working Policy*, but received little attention during the Paulsen era (1999-2010).[17]

Jan Paulsen (b. 1936), the first professional theologian to become the church's top leader, may perhaps be compared to Reuben Figuhr in his leadership emphases. Rather than stressing doctrinal and cultural uniformity, his ideal for the church was unity in diversity. But like Figuhr he was suspected by many of having liberal sympathies. And like Figuhr he was succeeded by someone who would start (and sustain) a crusade against the dangers the church was facing from those who were allegedly departing from 'the Truth' as we may discover it through a 'plain reading' of the Bible and a literal interpretation of the writings of Ellen G. White.

Since 2010 the church has been led by *Ted N.C. Wilson* (b. 1950). His re-election in July 2015 in San Antonio marked the beginning of his second term of office. While part of the church rejoiced, a considerable segment deplored the prospect of at least five more Wilson years. Probably more than any of his predecessors he has put his stamp of fundamentalist traditionalism on the church. It would seem that Wilson's re-election is also closely associated with the increasing North-South split in the church.

As soon as Ted N.C. Wilson had been elected General Conference president, he expressed his main burdens for the church in his significant sermon in Atlanta on July 3, 2010.[18] The title of his sermon *Go Forward* may well have been inspired by the 'Go Forward' message in the last volume of Ellen White's *Testimonies*.[19] This going forward was to be manifested in a number of different areas that since 'Atlanta' have become the staple of Wilson's messages at major meetings. The reception of this sermon was rather mixed, as has been the reaction to similar sermons at main church gatherings in the years that followed. Many were jubilant, but many others have listened with growing frustration. In fact, many have referred to Wilson as the most divisive Adventist church leader to date.

RECENT EMPHASES

The 'revival and reformation initiative' became one of Wilson's over-arching projects for the church in the five years of his first mandate. Of course, it is very difficult to evaluate in any objective and measurable way what results this initiative has produced. It is interesting to note, as already mentioned above, how very similar Wilson's call for revival and reformation was to that of President Robert Pierson.

Pierson was very concerned about the nearly two decades of alleged 'liberalizing' tendencies under President Reuben H. Figuhr, and he was determined to steer the church in another direction. Raymond Cottrell (1911-2003), a prominent editor of the *Review and Herald* and of the seven-volume *SDA Bible Commentary*, described Pierson in these words: 'Robert H. Pierson was a gracious person, a dedicated Adventist, a gentleman in every way, but also a person with clear objectives and resolute determination to achieve them.' He saw 'Pierson, Gordon M. Hyde and Gerhard Hasel as 'the three architects behind the decade of obscurantism (1969-1979).' According to Cottrell this 'triumvirate' attempted to gain full control of Adventist biblical studies in this decade.[20]

During the Annual Council (then named the Fall Council) of 1973 the Pierson administration launched a 'revival and reformation' project. Pierson proposed nine areas of special focus, as the church would concentrate on 'revival and reformation':
• An unprepared church.
• The message being subtly attacked through questioning the inspiration of the Bible and the Spirit of Prophecy.

- Institutions that need redirection by their board chairman and administration.
- Church leadership in need of revival and recommitment.
- A church drifting away from the study of God's Word—a need for a revival in Bible study.
- Homes that need help to cope with modern pressures—the importance of establishing the 'family altar.'
- Need for 'first-love' witnessing.
- Need for 'first-love' giving.
- Need for a revival of Bible-based preaching that stresses the theme of 'Christ our righteousness.'[21]

Pierson's book *Revival and Reformation*,[22] and his emotional farewell speech in 1973, after he resigned from the presidency for health reasons, expressed to a large extent the same concerns as have also been voiced over and over again by Ted N.C. Wilson. This somewhat lengthy quote from Robert Pierson is a clear illustration:

> *Regrettably, there are those in the church who belittle the inspiration of the total Bible, who scorn the first 11 chapters of Genesis, who question the Spirit of Prophecy's short chronology of the age of the earth, and who subtly and not so subtly attack the Spirit of Prophecy. There are some who point to the reformers and contemporary theologians as a source and the norm for Seventh-day Adventist doctrine. There are those who allegedly are tired of the hackneyed phrases of Adventism. There are those who wish to forget the standards of the church we love. There are those who covet and would court the favor of the evangelicals; those who would throw off the mantle of a peculiar people; and those who would go the way of the secular, materialistic world.*
>
> *Fellow leaders, beloved brethren and sisters—don't let it happen! I appeal to you as earnestly as I know how this morning—don't let it happen! I appeal to Andrews University, to the Seminary, to Loma Linda University—don't let it happen! We are not Seventh-day Anglicans, not Seventh-day Lutherans—we are Seventh-day Adventists! This is God's last church with God's last message!*[23]

Again, one cannot to fail to notice the great similarity between the 'revival and reformation' emphasis of Robert Pierson and that of Ted N.C. Wilson, a few decades later. In spite of frequent references to the role of the Holy Spirit, and the so-called 'latter rain,' the character of Wilson's revival and reformation emphasis has been very much determined by human programs that would help to bring this about. The administrative and organizational measures to promote this *revival and reformation* initiative beg the question whether perhaps too much is being orchestrated and too little left to the initiative of the Spirit himself. A committee was established at the General Conference level, and one of the vice-presidents was given special oversight of this initiative. Subsidiary initiatives were developed, such as a special website,[24] and facilities to assist the church members in bringing their Bible reading habits and their prayer life to a different level, such as the *Revived by His Word* plan[25] and the *777 Prayer Chain*.[26] During Wilson's second term in office this emphasis seems to have lost much of its initial vigor.

ORDINATION OF WOMEN

During the first five Wilson years the ordination of female pastors caught at least as much attention as the *Revival and Reformation* initiative. It would be unfair to say that Wilson's view on this issue was the sole determining factor in the church's struggle with this controversial point, but it was clear that Wilson was not prepared to use his influence for creating an atmosphere in which this issue could have been resolved in a different way that could have found broad acceptance in the church.

The question whether women may be ordained to any church office and to pastoral ministry and leadership positions in the Adventist Church has been a matter of intense discussion since the 1960s. In this ongoing debate theological, ethical, cultural and traditional elements play a role, besides, at times, issues of church policies and politics. For many it has remained rather strange that a church that proudly points to a woman as one of its co-founders—who herself consistently stressed the importance of women in church work— is so hesitant in accepting women as fully equal to men. It may be understandable that in some areas of the world accepting women in ministry as fully equal to men still meets strong cultural barriers, but in the Western world many church members simply cannot understand why their church lags so far behind the general ethical norm of the world around us.

The decades of discussion have led to situations that are increasingly hard to explain. In 1984 the church decided at long last that it is all right to ordain women elders, if the church in areas in the world believed this to be proper, and later (in 2000) the way was also opened for the ordination of deaconesses. In 1987 a new type of credential was instituted. Men and women who hold non-pastoral positions of responsibility in the church could receive a 'Commissioned Minister' credential. Soon this was also used for women in ministry. It gave them most of the privileges of ordained ministers, but with some notable exceptions. This new credential is only valid within the geographical area for which the church entity that 'commissions' the individual is responsible. The person who holds this credential cannot be elected as president of a conference, union or division— let alone of the General Conference! Of course, this stipulation lacks any theological basis and is just a matter of policy. When all is said and done, it remains difficult to understand why female *elders* and *deaconesses* may be ordained, while this is considered improper for female *ministers*. Are there different kinds or gradations of ordination? What theological rationale can possibly explain the current situation?

Through the years a series of committees studied the topic of women's ordination, the most recent one being the international *TOSC* (*Theology of Ordination Study Committee*). The majority of its one-hundred-plus members read and listened to numerous documents, and convened a number of times. No consensus could be reached, but a majority concluded that the ordination of women is, in fact, not a theological issue, but rather a matter of culture and church policy. This was also the conclusion of most of the reports of the *Biblical Research Committees* that function at the division level. Unfortunately all this material was mostly ignored during the discussions in San Antonio.

When the General Conference session met in San Antonio in July 2015 the delegates were presented with a question to which they could reply with a simple 'yes' or 'no': Would the church allow the world regions (divisions) to decide whether or not they would permit the ordination of women pastors in their part of the world?[27] After a passionate, and at times ugly, debate, 41.3 percent of the delegates voted 'yes' and 58.5 percent voted 'no,' with just a few abstentions. If Wilson had been willing to join Jan Paulsen, the previous president of the world church, in encouraging the delegates to permit this freedom to the various areas of the world, there is little doubt that the outcome would have been quite different and the 'yes' vote would most likely have carried the day.

In the debates prior to and during the General Conference Session a relatively new theological theory came to play an ever more important role—and no doubt we have not heard the last of it. I am referring to the unscriptural idea of 'male headship,' which suggests that there is a distinct order in levels of authority: God—Christ—man—woman. This theory originated in conservative Calvinistic circles in the United States and was imported into Adventism by Samuele Bacchiocchi (1938-2008), a conservative scholar and popular author, who, as a rule, chose to write about controversial issues. It is based on a particular way of reading the Bible that we will have to look at a bit more closely.

'PLAIN READING'

Many of the current controversies in the Adventist Church have to do with a particular way of reading and interpreting the Bible. From the beginning of his presidency Ted N.C. Wilson has stressed the 'plain' reading of the Bible, i.e. the importance of accepting the literal meaning of the text. He continuously reminds his audiences of the dangers of all forms of historical criticism and recommends the reading of a few recent books about the Bible, and how it is to be interpreted, which have been produced by the *Biblical Research Institute*.[28] No doubt Wilson's approach to Scripture has strengthened the ever-present fundamentalist tendencies in Adventism.

Combined with this insistence on as literal an interpretation of the Bible as possible, is Wilson's constant hammering on the importance of the writings of Ellen G. White and on the principle that these should be the main point of reference for anything we say about everything. This uncritical use of her writings, without much thought to original context, has been warmly applauded by many in the church but, at the same time, has been much criticized by others. Wilson's sermons tend to be loaded with quotations from Ellen White's writings, that— all protests to the contrary—often even seem to eclipse the role of the Bible.

The enthusiasm for the 'Spirit of Prophecy' (as the writings of Ellen White are often referred to) received a very dramatic expression in the worldwide campaign to distribute tens of millions of copies of the book *The Great Controversy* during the first Wilson period. This initiative also received a rather mixed reception. In some countries members were keen to participate, and special editions of the book were printed in large quantities. However, in many other places, only abridged editions were issued with selected chapters, to ensure that the public would not be bombarded with too much of the anti-Catholic material that forms an important part of the book. In some areas of the world—especially in the West—participation in the project was almost nil or limited to small groups of mostly immigrant members. Many deplored this campaign and regretted that world leadership would impose this on the church without considering the serious objections that had been voiced. It was seen as another top-down directive and as an illustration of how the church's top administration now has chosen to operate.

Reference has already been made to the *Biblical Research Institute (BRI)* that is connected with the head office of the world church. It was created in 1975 with the purpose of providing the church administration with theological advice in cases of doctrinal controversies, and to research matters of a theological nature. It lost its semi-independent status, when in 2010 it was directly linked to the office of the General Conference president, with its director as a vice-president of the church. Thus, from that point onwards, there would clearly be a stronger measure of presidential control of the activities of the BRI. The resident theologians who work in the BRI have usually been quite conservative, and this trend has clearly intensified in recent years—leading the church further on the path of fundamentalism and doctrinal rigidity.

THE *FUNDAMENTAL BELIEFS* AND CREATION

One of the important agenda items at the 2015 General Conference session was the revision of the twenty-eight *Fundamental Beliefs* of the church, with the substantial rewriting of the article on creation (article 6) and a reference to a 'global' flood (in article 8) as the most controversial aspects. The revision of the church's *Fundamental Beliefs* caused a lot of discussion prior to the meetings and during the meetings, and, no doubt, will continue to be discussed. Two aspects demand our special attention.

Firstly, there is the clear trend towards an ever more detailed definition of Adventist beliefs. This trend did not begin in San Antonio. Many, however, hope this development will soon end, and will—preferably— be reversed! A brief look at the history of the *Fundamental Beliefs* may offer some surprises to many church members. At first the Adventist believers refused to make any summary of what they believed. 'We have no creed but the Bible,' was their motto. Compiling a list of doctrines, it was felt, was a major step in the direction of 'Babylon.' It would bring all unprejudiced Bible study to a halt. History had abundantly proven that, once such a 'creed' is accepted, it is well nigh impossible to make changes! The early Adventists had escaped from the creedal strangleholds of the churches to which they had belonged, and they did not want to return to something similar! However, after some time this rigid standpoint proved no longer tenable. The general public was asking questions about the beliefs of the Adventist Church, which needed to be answered. In 1853 James White, one of the early Adventist leaders and the editor of the official denominational publications, published the first informal summary of Adventist beliefs. In 1872 the church published a little pamphlet in which a list of twenty-five 'fundamental principles' was offered. It was not intended 'to secure uniformity' or to provide 'a system of faith,' but was simply meant as 'a brief statement, of what is, and has been, with great unanimity held by Adventist believers.'[29] The aim was simply 'to meet inquiries' and 'to correct false statements.' It was not until 1931 that a further statement of beliefs was prepared. This 'Statement of Beliefs of Seventh-day Adventists,' listing twenty-two doctrinal points, served the church until 1980. It was replaced by a new statement of twenty-seven 'fundamental beliefs,' voted by the delegates to the General Conference session in Dallas (TX, USA). An additional point (no. eleven) was adopted in 2005. This resulted in the *twenty-eight* Fundamental Beliefs.

In spite of this development of the church's statement of beliefs, from an informal list to inform the external public about the main tenets of Adventism into a very detailed definition of the key Adventist doctrines that all members are expected to accept, the church continues to insist that it has no creed but the Bible. Clearly this has become a matter of semantics, for the *Fundamental Beliefs* statement increasingly functions as a creed and all members—and, more so, all church employees—are, at least in theory, expected to agree with every single one of these points. Many church members are very uneasy about this ongoing trend and wonder where it will end.

And then there is a second point. In recent years it became clear that there has been a decided push from top church leadership—the General Conference president in particular, together with a group of conservative theologians—to tighten some of the articles in the *Fundamental Beliefs*. The special focus was on article six, which deals with the creation of the world. The text that was adopted in 1980 was already problematic to many scientists and other church members, who felt that more space ought to be given for less literal interpretations of the creation and flood stories. This was, however, seen as a danger that needed to be addressed. Therefore, the statement needed to be so revised that any loophole, leaving the slightest room for some theistic form of evolution and for any interpretation that differed from a 'plain reading' of the text, would be closed.[30] Those who defended the new formulation were satisfied when the vote (not unexpectedly) went their way. But lots of people present in San

Antonio and around the globe—especially in the Western world—felt disappointed or worse. For many, introducing non-biblical language into the new text to underscore that the seven creation days were literal 24-hour days, that were part of a period we now refer to as a week, and to stress that creation was a 'recent' event, as was also a 'recent' 'global' flood, was another tragic example of the steady slide into an utterly fundamentalist reading of the Bible. They felt that the Adventist Church was making the same kind of tragic mistake as the Catholic Church had committed when calling Galileo a heretic.

We will have to say more, later in this book, about the role of doctrine in the church and in the life of the individual believer. Postmodern Christians are not very interested in doctrinal fine print, and they fiercely object to being forced into a straitjacket of a list of doctrines that they must give assent to, if they are to be accepted as members 'in regular standing.' More and more people hesitate to join the Adventist Church if they have to say 'yes' to all twenty-eight *Fundamental Beliefs*. In good postmodern fashion they want to compile their own list and feel they should have the freedom to do so. If that is not possible, they will not enter the baptismal font! And, increasingly, people who have joined the church at some point in the past are no longer convinced of the correctness and/or the relevancy of some points and wonder how many of 'the twenty-eight' one needs to accept in order to remain a *bona fide* Adventist.

ENEMY-THINKING

Among the things that many Adventists—and especially those 'on the margins' of the church—dislike is the continued focus on some external enemy. From its beginning Adventism has been distrustful of other religious bodies. Our prophetic scenario pointed to Babylon as the counterpart of God's true church. The Adventist Church was considered as 'God's last church,' the 'remnant' people of God in a world doomed to perdition. 'Babylon' would ultimately unite all other religious powers, in particular the Roman Catholic 'mother church' and her 'daughters,' the apostate Protestant denominations, which, together with occultism, would form the evil end-time counterfeit trinity. In recent decades it seemed that this thinking in terms of 'us' and 'them' was gradually being nuanced. Although the official prophetic standpoints were not changed, there was much less emphasis on them. Much of the rather vitriolic language of the past was toned down. The Adventist Church was more and more prepared to accept others as genuine Christians—albeit with 'less light' regarding biblical truth than 'the remnant church' had received. Although the Adventist Church did not want to join ecumenical organizations like the World Council of Churches, and discouraged national church entities from joining national councils of churches as formal members, there appeared to be a general willingness to co-operate with other Christians in a number of different areas and to engage in discussions and consultations.

In recent times the desire for a return to isolation seems once more to be gaining the upper hand. The church's president has repeatedly warned against reading non-Adventist theological books, having non-Adventist speakers address Adventist congregations, establishing close ecumenical contacts, and participating in training programs provided by other Christians. The media that are sponsored by such independent ministries as *3ABN, Amazing Facts, Amazing Discoveries,* and various non-official Adventist publishers, provide a continuous diet of alarmist and conspiracy-fueled end-time messages, in which the old-time fury against anything Catholic and ecumenical has been enthusiastically rekindled. For many Adventists 'on the margins'—as well as for many who are still firmly within the Adventist fold—this renewed enemy thinking is unpalatable. Many ask what this has to do with a gospel of grace and a Lord who has already conquered all evil powers and whose return is the hope that 'burns within our hearts.'

HOMOSEXUALITY

The list of concerns of those who are 'on the margins' of the church must remain incomplete, but one major ethical issue must still be mentioned. We have already seen that many members in the Western world find it very difficult to understand the church's attitude towards the ordination of woman to the gospel ministry. It has led some to leave the church. They do not want to belong to an organization that continues to discriminate against women and they believe there are no valid theological arguments to do so. On the contrary, they believe the gospel of Christ demands full gender equality.

Many Adventists in the Western world find it also increasingly difficult to accept the church's position on homosexuality and same-sex relationships. This is especially true for young people, but the unease with the denominational standpoint is found among men and women of all age groups. They meet gay and lesbian people; they work with them as colleagues and have them among their friends. Some have gay or lesbian siblings. Many also know of gays and lesbians and people with yet other sexual orientations in the Adventist Church, and are keenly aware of their struggle to be fully accepted.

In past years the Adventist Church has published a number of unfortunate statements in which homosexuality has been listed as one of a series of serious sexual aberrations.[31] More recently, church leaders have emphasized the importance of interacting with gays and lesbians in a loving and pastoral way. At the same time the church has not left the members in any doubt that, whereas having a homosexual *orientation* is not sin, any homosexual *activity* is totally unacceptable. The only option for homosexuals is to remain celibate.

According to the official view of the church, a literal reading of the so-called 'anti-homo-texts' that are found in the Bible[32] will lead to the unambiguous conclusion that a Christian must abstain from any homosexual activities and cannot enter into a same-sex relationship. However, others argue that these texts can also be read and interpreted in a different light and that the Bible never addresses the kind of same-sex relationships that we see today (between two men or two women, who love each other and want to be faithful to their partner for as long as they live). For many, again in particular for those 'on the margins' of the church, it is impossible to accept that homosexuals are often barely tolerated in the Adventist Church and seen (at best) as second-class members, who—even if they are baptized—cannot be trusted with any major church office.

THE LARGER PICTURE

The previous chapter has pointed to the crisis in contemporary Christianity and this chapter to a number of controversial issues in today's Adventism. I have no hesitancy in speaking of a real *crisis*. Not all will agree with this assessment and some will probably criticize my analysis of what is happening in the church. An all too common approach is to zero in on one or two details of a particular argument, find some points that they consider questionable, and then conclude that the total picture is unreliable. I would urge the reader first and foremost to look at the total picture and then decide whether this indeed fairly reflects reality. I believe it does.

The recent trends that I have described cause an often slow but steady exodus from the church. As we continue to address the enormous challenges of this crisis in the Adventist Church, and in the next chapter look in some detail at the crisis of faith that many Adventist believers experience, it is important to realize that all of this does not happen in a vacuum. What happens in the Adventist Church is, to a large extent, a reflection of what is happening in major parts of contemporary Western Christianity.

And, as we go along, we must keep three other elements in mind. (1) Trends in the Adventist Church of today cannot be detached from its past history. Without some knowledge of our history we cannot see things in the right perspective; (2) many of the issues that play a major role in the current crisis in Adventism are a matter of *hermeneutics,* i.e. of how to read and interpret the Bible; and (3) *change is possible.* In the course of Adventist history many things have changed—some for the better and some for the worse. Further change for the better (from my perspective) is possible. The church can change to a less fundamentalist approach to the Bible. Leadership can become less controlling and can allow, or even stimulate, diversity in the way we practice our faith in different parts of the world, in our many different cultures. And we do not need to be so rigid in our doctrinal convictions as is often suggested, if we want to remain 'real' Adventists!

Numerous things have changed in the church, but many of these changes worry rather than please most 'believers on the margins.' It will be clear from what follows that I hope for the kind of change that will bring a breath of fresh air—an *aggiornamento*—into my church. My conviction that this kind of change is possible is one of the main reasons why I have written this book. But real change often takes a lot of time and therefore requires patience. A cursory study of church history confirms the fact that most changes have had a long incubation time. But they will eventually come, if enough people want these changes and allow the Spirit of the Lord to bring them about.

1 http://docs.adventistarchives.org/docs/ASR/ASR2014.pdf#view=fit.

2 David F. Wells, *Above Earthly Powers: Christ in a Postmodern World* (Grand Rapids, MI: Wm. B. Eerdmans, 2005), pp. 108, 109.

3 Frank S. Mead, *Handbook of Denominations in the United States* (13th edition; Nashville, TN: Abingdon Press, 2010).

4 See Richard W. Schwartz and Floyd Greenleaf, *Light Bearers: A History of the Seventh-day Adventist Church* (Nampa, ID: Pacific Press, 2000 rev. ed.), pp. 615-625.

5 http://www.bwanet.org.

6 George R. Knight, *A Search for Identity: The Development of Seventh-day Adventist Beliefs* (Hagerstown, MD: Review and Herald, 2000), pp. 17-21.

7 David O. Moberg, *Church as Social Institution* (Upper Saddle River, NJ.: Prentice Hall, 1962; revised 1984).

8 Cf. the title of his book *Why Christianity Must Change or Die* (San Francisco, CA: HarperCollins, 1998).

9 Some of the remarks in the following paragraphs reflect the presentation I gave to the German AWA (*Adventistischer Wissenschaftlicher Arbeitskreis*)—an organization not unlike the Forum Associations in the United States—October 2-4, 2015, in Eisenach, Germany.

10 Audio recording of Gilbert Valentine's presentation on July 25, 2015 in Glendale, CA, at the SDA Forum meeting: http://spectrummagazine.org/sites/default/files/LApercent20Forumpercent20-percent20Gilpercent20Valentine.mp3

11 Alternative spellings are frequently used: 'Christian Connexion' or 'Christian Connexxion.'

12 George R. Knight, ed., *Seventh-day Adventists Answer Questions on Doctrine*, annotated edition (Berrien Springs, MI: Andrews University Press, 2003).

13 The *Seventh-day Adventist Bible Commentary*, 7 vols. (Washington, DC: Review and Herald, 1953-1957. For the historical background of this project, see Raymond F. Cottrell, 'The Untold Story of the Bible Commentary,' *Spectrum* Vol. 16, no. 3 (August 1985), 35–51.

14 See my paper 'Revival and Reformation—a current Adventist Initiative in a broader perspective,' presented at the European Theological Teachers' Convention, Newbold College, UK), March 25-29, 1915. Published in Jean-Claude Verrecchia, ed., *Ecclesia Reformata, Semper Reformanda: Proceedings of the European Theology Teachers' Convention 25-28 March 2015* (Newbold Academic Press, 2016), pp. 101-121.

15 For the original text of the 27 Fundamental Beliefs, see e.g. Ministerial Association of Seventh-day Adventists, *Seventh-day Adventists Believe—A Biblical Exposition of the 27 Fundamental Doctrines* (General Conference of SDA, 1988).

16 See for a biography: Milton Hook, *Desmond Ford: Reformist Theologian, Gospel Revivalist* (Riverside, CA: Adventist Today Foundation, 2008).

17 See *General Conference Working Policy*, A15; also: https://www.adventist.org/en/information/official-statements/documents/article/go/0/total-commitment-to-god.

18 For a transcript of this sermon, see *Adventist Review, GC Session Bulletin no. 8.*, July 9, 2010.

19 Ellen G. White, *Testimonies for the Church*, vol. 9 (Mountain View, CA: Pacific Press, 1948 ed.). p. 271.

20 http://en.wikipedia.org/wiki/Raymond_Cottrell.

21 *Minutes General Conference Committee*, October 15, 1973. http://documents.adventistarchives.org/Minutes/GCC/GCC1973-10a.pdf

22 Robert H. Pierson, *Revival and Reformation* (Washington DC: Review and Herald, 1974).

23 Robert H. Pierson, 'Final Appeal to God's People,' *Review and Herald*, 26 October 1973.

24 http://www.revivalandreformation.org/.

25 http://revivedbyhisword.org/.

26 http://www.revivalandreformation.org/777.

27 The question was formulated as follows: 'After your prayerful study on ordination from the Bible, the writings of Ellen G. White, and the reports of the study commissions; and after your careful consideration of what is best for the church and the fulfillment of its mission, is it acceptable for division executive committees, as they may deem it appropriate in their territories, to make provision for the ordination of women to the gospel ministry? Yes or No.'

28 *Understanding Scripture: An Adventist Approach*, Biblical Research Institute Studies, vol. 1 (2006); *Interpreting Scripture: Bible Questions and Answers*, Biblical Research Institute Studies, vol. 2 (2010).

29 'Seventh-day Adventist Doctrinal Statements,' in: Don F. Neufeld, ed., *Seventh-day Adventist Encyclopedia* (Hagerstown, MD: Review and Herald, 1996 ed.), vol. 2, p. 464.

30 Article 6 of the Fundamental Beliefs, on creation, is now worded as follows: God is Creator of all things, and has revealed in Scripture the authentic and historical account of His creative activity. In a recent six-day creation the Lord made 'the heavens and the earth, the sea and all that is in them' and rested on the seventh day. Thus He established the Sabbath as a perpetual memorial of His creative work performed and completed during six literal days that together with the Sabbath constituted a week as we experience it today. The first man and woman were made in the image of God as the crowning work of Creation, given dominion over the world, and charged with responsibility to care for it. When the world was finished it was 'very good,' declaring the glory of God. (Gen. 1-2; Ex. 20:8-11; Ps. 19:1-6; 33:6, 9; 104; Isa. 45:12; Acts 17:24; Col. 1:16; Heb. 11:3; Rev. 10:6; 14:7.)

31 E.g. in the statements 'Homosexuality,' and 'A Statement of Concern on Sexual Behavior' in: *Statements, Guidelines and Other Documents of the Seventh-day Adventist Church* (Silver Spring, MD: Communication Department of the General Conference of Seventh-day Adventists, 2006), pp. 38, 94-95. A cover story in Ministry magazine in the 1980s announced that Adventists had found a way to 'heal' homosexuals. The exposure that came on the heels of that left the publishers shame-faced.

32 The most important texts that are cited by those who insist that the Bible does not allow for any homosexual activity are: Deuteronomy 23:17, 18; Leviticus 18:22; Genesis 19; Judges 19; Romans 1:20, 21; 1 Corinthians 6:9 and 1 Timothy 1:8-10.

CHAPTER 4

Is there a God? Really?

I was ten years old. For some time Henk, my little brother, about two years my junior, had not been well, but our local family doctor could not find much wrong with him. Then, quite suddenly, the symptoms became so serious that immediate hospitalization was required. Two weeks later Henk was dead. A form of rheumatic heart disease had not been diagnosed in time, with fatal results. Our family was not very well to do, to put it mildly, and he was therefore buried in an unmarked grave in the cemetery of the village where we lived. I can still see the school class around the open grave, singing for their classmate, and I remember the sermon by one of our favorite Adventist pastors, who had come from Amsterdam to conduct the service.

I believed in God in my own childish way. In the few days between the moment when the coffin was carried into our small house—where it stood for four days with an open lid in the rather narrow hallway, where we had to pass it all the time—and the funeral, I prayed fervently. I knew the Bible stories in which dead people had miraculously been restored to life. I realized that this had only happened occasionally, and that most dead people remained dead, but it had happened a few times and I prayed that God would also make an exception for my brother. It did not seem reasonable that he would no longer be with us. Why did God do this to us? In spite of my pleas, God did not make an exception. Why not? Why did he let Henk die?

Only a few years later we stood in the same cemetery, this time to bid a final farewell to my father. He lived to the age of fifty. After a rather complicated life, with a lot of illness, and after several serious misfortunes and setbacks, he had developed leukemia. The uneven struggle with this cancerous disease lasted about six years—a tough period for him and the entire family. My father was no more. I was fourteen and would have to grow up without a father. In fact, even in the years prior to his death, I did not really have a caring father like most boys of my age. I have always missed the intimate bond with a real father in my life. Why did this happen to me? And to my mother, to my sisters? Why did God allow this? Did he not know that we believed in him? Why did he ignore us and why did he not help us?

A few decades later—I was now around forty—my youngest sister died, aged 32, leaving a husband and three small children behind. A vicious brain tumor had done its quick and deadly work. It was a shock, and left me questioning, Why did God allow this to happen to a young family? How would these kids cope without a mother? Why, God, why?

Most of us will experience moments or even extended periods of suffering, or have already gone through difficult times in our personal past. We realize that none of us is immortal, and that one day we will lose our elderly parents and other older relatives and friends. But we will never get used to losing people who are taken from us in mid-life, or to the sight of small children who are dying of cancer.

I realize that many people had a much tougher life than I have had so far. And, when I think of the countless victims of war situations, who must live on, with a lifelong trauma, without parents, or without their partner and their children, words remain empty when I seek to describe what they must feel. Why does an almighty God allow such atrocities?

In his 1974 bestselling book *When Bad Things Happen to Good People*, Rabbi Harold Kushner suggested that we may be able to accept some suffering as the inevitable part of human life, but that the fact that there is so much inexplicable suffering leaves us baffled. This is even more true when we look not only at the suffering of individuals, but also at suffering on a much larger scale—the misery of entire communities or nations. Think of the natural disasters that hit our planet with an uncanny frequency, the earthquakes that bury many thousands of innocent people under the rubble of their houses and factories, the tsunamis and typhoons that cause terrible devastation and leave millions of people dead or homeless. Why do such things happen?

Acts of terrorism bring massive suffering and disrupt our lives. We can no longer board a plane unless we have first emptied our pockets and thrown our half-empty water bottles in the trash bin, and have passed through a body scan; we find metal detection gates at the entrances of major public buildings, and we are filmed by surveillance cameras dozens of times every day. I read a recent report that in the United Kingdom a person who walks for a day through the streets of London will be filmed at least 300 times. Nonetheless, terrorists still succeed in making their cruel point by randomly killing men, women and children, who simply happen to be at the wrong place at the wrong time. Why does all this happen? Why can IS and Boka Haram, the drug cartels in South-America and other terrorist organizations, continue their appalling practices?

Why did our world experience worldwide wars with their tens of millions of victims? Anyone who knows a little bit of history has not only heard of the 'Great War' of 1914-1918 and of the Second World War, the Vietnam War, the 'killing fields' of the Cambodian Khmer Rouge in the late 1970s, and the genocide in Rwanda in 1994, but also of the more recent atrocities in Sudan, Yemen, and Iraq, et cetera. And then there is the suffering in many other, sometimes conveniently forgotten, wars around the globe. As I write this chapter the terrible events in Syria have already claimed hundreds of thousands of lives. And so it goes on.

BUT WHY?

In the previous two chapters we discussed the deep crisis of contemporary Christianity and the widespread distrust in the institutional church. However, the crisis goes far deeper than an increasing loss of confidence in the church as an organization.

Many of those who find themselves 'on the margins' of the church experience a crisis of personal faith. Of course, these two things are closely connected, but the crisis of faith reaches far deeper than just a strongly reduced confidence in the church. It affects our lives at the most profound level.

A great many Christians, with their roots in the wide variety of denominations across the religious spectrum—from ultra-left to extreme-right and everything in between—experience a crisis in their faith. Of course, this is not a new phenomenon, but at present it seems to be much more intense than ever before. It is not restricted to any specific age group. And let no one for a moment think Adventists are immune to this crisis. Many young Adventists are not wondering what exactly happens before, during and after the thousand-year period of Revelation 20, or how they may extract the 1844 date from Daniel 8 and 9. They want to know whether there really is a God and, if so, why all these terrible things happen in the world and in the society of which they are a part. The tragedy is that they may find quite a few people in the church who are ready to give them a series of lengthy Bible studies to sort out questions about the doctrinal fine print, but who are unable to address seriously the real problems that trouble their soul. They, as well as many folks of previous generations, are 'on the margins' of the church, because they have been disappointed about the things people in their church say and do, and because of trends they see in their church. But often their soul-searching goes much deeper. They wonder, *Does God really exist?* And if he does, how can we reconcile all this suffering and misery in the world with an almighty God? So often, so many of us echo the question that became the title of Philip Yancey's inspiring book, *Where is God when it hurts?*

GOD—ALL-POWERFUL AND LOVING?

One of the most crucial questions many Christians are struggling with is, How do we reconcile the love of God with the fact that he is supposed to be all-powerful? When Christians try to explain what God is like, they will often quote the simple, three-word biblical definition: *God is love* (1 John 4:6). God is love in the purest possible form.

This, the Bible tells us, was sublimely manifested in the gift of God's Son, Jesus Christ, who came to bring salvation to us. But speaking about God also involves his other attributes: God is *eternal* (he has always existed and will always exist); he knows everything (he is omniscient); he can be at all places at the same time (he is *omnipresent*); and he never changes (he is *immutable*). *But he is also all-powerful (omnipotent):* this means that there is no limit to what he can do. He is portrayed in the Bible as the Creator of the universe and of everything it comprises. And we are told that he has the power to create 'a new heaven and a new earth' when history, as we now know it, comes to an end.

So, there you have the dilemma that millions of people—including large numbers of Seventh-day Adventist Christians—cannot solve: If God is total love and has unlimited power, why is there all this suffering? Why does God not intervene and protect the creatures he supposedly loves? We would like to say to God, 'We challenge you to explain this! Defend yourself! Help us understand why you just seem to sit and wait, rather than intervene and stop all evil and destruction, and get us out of the mess that we so often find ourselves in.'

This reflects the experience of Steve Jobs, the genius and co-founder of the *Apple* imperium, who died of cancer in 2011. In his youth most Sundays Jobs attended a Lutheran church, but he lost his faith at the age of thirteen. He asked his Sunday School teacher, 'If I raise my finger, will God know which one I am going to raise even before I do it?' When the pastor answered with: 'Yes, God knows everything,' Steve pulled the cover of the July 1968 *Life* magazine out of his pocket. This shocking cover showed a pair of starving children in Biafra (Nigeria). He then asked the pastor whether God also knew of these children. The only answer Steve received was, 'Steve, I know you don't understand, but yes, God knows about that.' Steve Jobs could not be satisfied with this answer and left the church, never to return.[1]

Theologians have a technical term for this topic. They speak of *theodicy.* This word is derived from two Greek words: *theos* and *dike* —

God and *justice*. In other words: How does God justify his apparent inaction when we suffer? Surfing the Internet I found the following succinct and helpful definition of *theodicy*: 'The defense of God's goodness and omnipotence in view of the existence of evil.'[2]

For lots of people reconciling God's love with his unlimited power is an unanswerable question that leads them to conclude, There is no loving God! However, thinkers of all times and all places have refused to accept this fatalistic conclusion and have tried to find an answer that would satisfy them. I have read quite a few of their often quite complicated books on *theodicy*. Perhaps the most readable and informative book about this topic that I have come across in recent times is Richard Rice's book *Suffering and the Search for Meaning*. The subtitle clarifies further what Rice sets out to do: to give *Responses to the Problem of Pain*.

Dr Rice, a theology professor at Loma Linda University in California, expects no extensive theological knowledge on the part of his readers. In his very accessible book Rice provides a survey of various approaches to the why-question, which I will briefly summarize.[3] The first view is that every attempt to justify God must fail; we cannot possibly find a way to reconcile the misery in the world with the existence of an almighty and loving God.

It has, however, been argued in at least five different ways that a solution to the why-question is possible.
1. We may start from the idea that all suffering and misery is, in some mysterious way, part of God's plan for humankind. Admittedly, we often do not understand why God would approve or allow many of the events that occur. But he makes no mistakes and we must trust that in his time all things will fall into place.
2. God is not to blame for the fact that there is so much suffering in the world. It is the result of man's free will. God did not want robots, but created beings that would love and serve him from their own free will. God took the risk that things might turn sour, but this does not make him responsible for our wrong choices and, therefore, for all the suffering we see in the world.

3. We may not be able to find explanations for all the suffering that we see and experience, but we can appreciate the fact that most things that happen to us have the potential to stimulate our inner growth and to help us to mature spiritually.

4. A cosmic conflict between good and evil is raging, and human beings play a role in this struggle between the powers of light and darkness. Seventh-day Adventist Christians have traditionally opted for this perspective and refer to this cosmic conflict as 'the great controversy.'

5. Then, finally, there are those who opt for a different kind of response. They tell us we should revise our point of departure. God is not omniscient and not all-powerful in the classical sense of those terms. They say that God does not know exactly how we will decide to use our free will, and he does not have the possibility of intervening when we make wrong decisions.[4]

The book by Richard Rice is of great value because it provides such a lucid survey of the various options and then deals with the strong and the weak points of each of these approaches. It receives much added value through the way in which the author also deals with the personal dimension of the problem. Human suffering, he says, is not just a philosophical and theological *problem* (in fact, he prefers the term *'mystery'*). Sooner or later it affects all of us very personally. Rice proposes that we might combine aspects of the various approaches as we try to distill 'fragments of meaning,' and hope to find comfort and support when we are struck by personal disaster.

Personally, just like Rice, I also see value in several of the suggested 'solutions.' I am particularly attracted to the more unorthodox view of point number five, but I will not allow myself to be drawn into a long discussion of this topic. As a pastor and as someone with a professional theological interest, I would find such a discussion very interesting. At the same time I realize that for most people the *why*-question will not be solved by any academic debate. Whatever arguments we may put forward, it simply does not 'feel good' that a loving God, who is all-powerful, does not prevent or stop the suffering we personally experience and the misery we see every evening in the news on our TV screens. If there is an answer, for most of us it will not primarily be based on rational arguments. We will need to return to this at a later point.

INTELLECTUAL DOUBT

Throughout the history of Christendom many people have doubted the existence of God, while others have done everything possible to 'prove' that the Christian God must exist.[5] These 'proofs' usually followed a similar pattern: Every effect must have a cause, and this cause must also have its own cause, and so on. Ultimately, there must be a First Cause at the beginning of everything: *God.* Others have developed this line of thinking further by arguing that, if we can actually form an idea about a God who is eternal, almighty and all-knowing, this in itself proves that there is such a God, for an idea like this cannot simply emerge from a limited human mind, unless it is caused by a Cause (with a capital C). Also, we are reminded that some general moral laws seem to be widely shared by humankind; this can only be explained, it is argued, by the fact that there is a supreme Moral Being who has somehow implanted these moral principles in the human race.

The most famous 'argument' for God's existence ran like this: If we trek through the forest and suddenly discover a house with a well-kept garden, we will assume that someone must have built the house and laid out the garden. Or, if we consider the intricate clockwork of a watch, we do not speculate that the watch might have come about through some kind of mysterious spontaneous generation or some 'big bang' in the distant past. We assume that a watchmaker of flesh and blood has been at work. Likewise, when we study the universe and see a definite order, we cannot reasonably avoid the conclusion that there must be a Maker who has put the cosmos and the world in that particular order. Whenever there is evidence of *design* we must postulate a *designer!* While this argument from design lost much of its power when Charles Darwin and other evolutionists proposed their theories of a gradual evolution of the various species of plant and animal life, in recent years it has made an interesting comeback among some Christian scholars.

Few people today find the traditional 'proofs' for God's existence very convincing. Many Christians who are firmly convinced that God exists, do, in fact, admit that no absolute proof is possible! However, although it may be difficult, or even impossible, to provide absolute proof for God's existence, *proving that there is no God is even more difficult!* Just consider this simple illustration. Providing solid evidence that there are rhinos in the world is not too difficult. You can find rhinos in any major zoo! However, if you want to have definitive proof that *blue* rhinos do not exist, this would be much more challenging, if not impossible. You would have to investigate whether anywhere in the world, including the most remote and inaccessible places, a blue rhino may be found. As long as you have not searched the entire world, you cannot be absolutely sure!

In most cases intellectual doubt with regard to the existence of God does not disappear by trying to 'prove' that he is alive and well. It will need a different approach, as we will see. In the meantime we must not forget another major hurdle for many who are struggling with their faith.

WHY CHRISTIANITY?

The Western world is no longer solidly Christian. People with non-Christian religions have come to live among us, and many of us have traveled to places where we have been confronted with Islam, Hinduism, Buddhism or some other non-Christian faith. As a result many are now asking the question, If there is a God, who is he? Is he the God of the Christians or perhaps the Allah of the Muslims? Or are there perhaps many gods as, for instance, Hinduism teaches?

How can Christians be so sure that their religion is better than all other religions? What criteria do they have to determine that their religion is the true one, or at least superior to the others? Could it not be that all religions are of equal value? Are they perhaps all equally valid ways of finding a deeper meaning in life? Does it really matter whether you call the highest being 'God' or address him as 'Allah'? Does it make an essential difference whether you get your inner rest from Buddha or from Jesus Christ? Does it matter whether you worship in a Hindu temple or burn a candle in a Catholic cathedral? Are not all religions trying to do same: establish a connection between us and the unknown Beyond? These questions are yet another reason for widespread doubt.

Or, on the other hand, are those people right who say that all religions are the product of human imaginings, and nothing more?

QUESTIONS ABOUT THE BIBLE

Many who still believe in God, and who are more attracted to Christianity than to any other religion, struggle with their understanding of the Bible. This is especially true for people who grew up in a denomination with a rather literalistic approach to the Bible. If the Bible tells them that a man survived a lengthy stay in the belly of a big fish, and that a snake and a donkey spoke in human language, this must actually have happened! But to many, a lot of the things they were willing to accept in the past are not so clear-cut for them in their later years. This is also true for many Seventh-day Adventists. Although the Seventh-day Adventist Church officially rejects the label of fundamentalism, and Adventist theology claims that it does not accept the theory of verbal inspiration, in actual practice things are quite different.

Maybe we should first say a few words about these two terms, *fundamentalism* and *verbal inspiration*. Nowadays the term 'fundamentalism' is used rather broadly. The authoritative *Merriam-Webster Dictionary* defines 'fundamentalism' as 'a movement or attitude stressing strict and literal adherence to a set of basic principles' and then mentions 'political fundamentalism' and 'Islamic fundamentalism' as prime examples of this usage. However, the first and primary definition that is given is more specific: 'A movement of twentieth-century Protestantism emphasizing the literally interpreted Bible as fundamental to Christian life and teachings.'

The movement of Fundamentalism (usually spelled with a capital F) arose in the first quarter of the twentieth century. A group of theologians, who were horror-struck by the ever more influential liberal trends in many denominations in North America, decided to write a series of brochures to combat what they saw as a deadly threat to American Protestantism. These pamphlets became known as the 'fundamentals'—and this inspired the term fundamentalism.

Verbal inspiration is the theory of inspiration that maintains that *every single word* is inspired. It is admitted that this would only apply to the exact wording of the original documents (in Hebrew, Aramaic and Greek), but the main thesis is that the biblical authors were mere scribes who wrote down what the Spirit told them. Because every word was 'dictated' to them by the Spirit, God's Word cannot contain any errors (it is, in other words, *infallible*). The Bible is in all things historically totally reliable. And when the Bible conflicts with science, the Bible always wins.

Before the 1920s Adventists had gradually moved towards a theory of 'thought' inspiration, the idea that the authors communicated the ideas that God gave them in their own human words, and through using their own style of writing. Ellen. G. White was among those who supported this view.[6] During the famous 'Bible Conference' of 1919 key Adventist leaders also spoke in favor of this idea.[7] However, when the Fundamentalist movement gained increasing strength in the United States, it soon also affected the Adventist Church, and the 'verbal inspiration' theory became quite dominant, both with respect to the origin of the Bible as with regard to the nature of the writings of the prophet, Ellen G. White. Through the years the fundamentalist streak in Adventism at times somewhat abated. But it has remained a continuing problem (at least, that is how I see it), and it has resurged in full force in recent times. For a large group of Adventists this trend towards fundamentalism, with its narrow interpretation of inspiration, has become increasingly unpalatable.

Three aspects of the Bible have created special uneasiness on the part of many Christian—including Seventh-day Adventist—Bible readers: (1) the violence and cruelty in the Old Testament; (2) the statements that conflict with science and common sense; (3) the miracle stories—including those of the resurrection and the ascension of Jesus.

The Koran is presently under frequent and heavy attack. Politicians and the media often describe it as the source that inspires 'radical' Islam, with its holy war (*jihad*) against non-Muslims, its merciless *Sharia*-law and its systematic discrimination against women. However, the argument does not stop at this point, for it is often emphasized that the Bible contains just as much cruelty and, like the Koran, condones violence and even genocide. Or, even more pointedly, it is stressed that it was the God of the Bible himself who, time and again, ordered the slaughter of men, women and children!

Indeed, even those who (try to) adhere to a rather fundamentalist view of the Bible must admit that some lengthy sections in the Old Testament do not make for very pleasant reading. The details of what happened are, at times, definitely gruesome. I have not done the arithmetic myself, but someone has and has reported the result on the Internet. I quote: 'Just about every other page in the Old Testament has God killing somebody! ... In total God kills 371,186 people directly, and orders another 1,862,265 people murdered.'[8] It is not difficult to draw some examples from this chronicle of violent death. God drowned the entire population of the earth, leaving only eight people alive (Genesis 7:21-23); just before the exodus of the people of Israel from Egypt, God decided to kill all firstborn Egyptian children, because the pharaoh was so stubborn (Exodus 12:29); in 1 Samuel 6:19 we read how God killed 50.000 men because they dared to peek into the ark of the covenant; and in 2 Kings 23, 24 we find the gruesome story of how God killed a group of children who had made fun of the prophet Elisha. And so on.

And what to think of a story like that of Abraham, who was ordered by God to sacrifice his son Isaac? For Larry King, who for decades presented the popular *Larry King Live* show, this disqualified God forever.[9]

And what do we do with the story of the Judge Jephthah who was ready to sacrifice his daughter, because he had made a rash promise to God (Judges 11:30-39)? And speaking of sacrifices, what kind of God enjoys the killing of tens of thousands of animals for his honor and glory?

According to 2 Chronicles 7:5 King Solomon, at the occasion of the dedication of the temple which he had built in Jerusalem, offered twenty-two thousand head of cattle and a hundred and twenty thousand sheep and goats! Can you picture a slaughter on such an unimaginable scale?

CREATION

Few scholars have so ferociously attacked the creation and flood stories, as told in the Bible, as the British scientist Richard Dawkins. The following quote leaves us in no uncertainty about his view of the Bible: 'The Bible should be taught, but emphatically not as reality. It is fiction, myth, poetry, anything but reality.'[10] Maarten 't Hart, a Dutch novelist (with a professional background in biology!) has essentially the same message for his readers. His recent book about his mother[11] has a chapter about a discussion he had with her about Noah's ark. Not only is it extremely amusing to read, but it is a good illustration of the kind of questions many Bible readers have. When Maarten 't Hart writes about religion and faith, apart from being very cynical he also demonstrates an extensive knowledge of the Bible and often puts forward arguments that leave many of his readers wondering about the veracity of the biblical narrative. He tried to convince his mother that her literal reading of the Flood story was totally ridiculous. He told her he had made some calculations regarding Noah's ark. The Bible indicates that this ship was large enough for all animals, 'after their kind'—one pair of all 'unclean' animals and seven pairs of all 'clean' animals. According to Maarten, the world is the habitat of roughly two million 'kinds,' and therefore tens of millions of animals must have entered the ark through a narrow door, in an impossibly brief period. But leaving this mind-boggling fact aside, How did these animals make their way to the ark? Some kinds of snails are only found in Scandinavia. They travel a maximum of about five meters a day, which means that the journey must have taken them at least a few years. But then there is the further complication that they have only a short life span and must have died while en route. And how about feeding all these animals during the sea voyage? Moreover, how did Noah make sure the animals did not kill each other during their cruise? And then, just think of all the manure. Et cetera, et cetera.

Of course, Maarten 't Hart's definition of the term 'kind' may not be the same as the one used by the writer of the Bible story, but he echoes the kind of doubt many readers of the Genesis story cannot easily shake off.

Some time ago I visited Australia and, of course, I was keen to see kangaroos. The kangaroo is just one of a large variety of marsupials. The fact that these creatures are only found in Australia causes numerous scientific problems and made me wonder about the biblical stories of a creation and a worldwide Flood. I could not help wondering how these animals would have hopped from 'down under' to the Middle East, and back again to Australia. Even if there was no water barrier before the Flood, there certainly must have been one after such a Deluge as is described in the Bible. I know I am not the only person in the Adventist Church who has such questions.

Many young people feel confused when they start secondary school and hear about evolution. Some will boldly tell their biology teachers that they have it all wrong and that they are not going to believe this (so-called scientific) rubbish. They want to stay with what they have heard from their parents and were told in church: that God created the world in just six short days. Therefore, all these modern ideas about slow evolution over millions of years cannot be true! But many of their peers are not so sure. Could it be that science is right, after all? What they read in their biology books sounds so much more logical than what they find in their Bible. Moreover, it seems that most people who have given the matter some serious thought have become convinced that the biblical story may indeed be a beautiful story, but must be regarded as myth rather than as history. Can all these highly educated people be wrong?

This is not something that only affects teenagers who have grown up in a Christian milieu, and are gradually becoming more critical and no longer accept something just because their parents say so and because their pastor insists that they must simply believe what the Bible says. I personally know quite a few people, even of my own age, who have believed in the creation story for most of their lives, but at some point admitted to themselves (and sometimes to others) that they are not so sure any more, and that they have become skeptical about a literal reading of the first few chapters of the Bible. They have concluded that there are simply too many loose ends. For instance, all of humanity supposedly has the same two ancestors, Adam and Eve. So, how do we explain that the world is populated by peoples of different races? And where do the brontosaurus and the tyrannosaurus rex and the other types of dinosaurs fit into the story?

Lots of other questions arise in the minds of many people. Did all the misery and suffering in the world really result from eating one fruit in a beautiful garden? And, by the way, why is the creation story told twice—in Genesis 1 and in Genesis 2? What do we do with the significant discrepancies between the two versions?

I know there are answers to these and to many other questions. And some people will be satisfied when they hear these answers and will happily push their doubts away. But for a lot of doubters the answers seem too simplistic and unconvincing, and, often, for each problem that is solved, ten others pop up.

MIRACLES

Just a week before I was writing the first draft of this chapter I attended a one-day symposium of the church historical society of which I am a member. The day was devoted to medieval miracle stories. It was fascinating to listen to two experts in medieval church history, as they made presentations about aspects of the medieval belief in miracle stories and of the way these stories tell us many things about the time in which they originated. I knew some of the stories they referred to, but some were new to me. I had never heard of the miracle of the bread that changed into a stone. This miracle allegedly happened in the Dutch city of Leyden in 1316. In that year the fields produced hardly any crops, which caused a severe famine in the city. A woman had somehow been able to get hold of a loaf of bread. After cutting it in two parts, she ate one half and hid the other half in her cupboard. Her next-door neighbor discovered this and pleaded with her to give her part of the bread. The owner of the bread refused to share it. It caused a bitter conflict between the two women. Finally, the woman who had hidden the bread cried out that she wished God would change the bread into a stone. God promptly answered her plea. The bread-turned-stone may still be seen in the *Lakenhal,* the beautiful museum of the city of Leyden.

Few people today would give much credence to such miracle stories. They just do not fit with our experience of how things work. Through the centuries there have been many who have also been very skeptical about the miracle stories that abound in the Bible—both in the Old and in the New Testament. The number of skeptics has been steadily increasing as we have learned more about the laws of nature and have found rational explanations for many phenomena that, in the past, were seen as miraculous coincidences. The miracle stories in the Bible do not seem to align with our everyday life. When we have dropped something in a river or canal, there is no prophet at hand to help us in getting the item back, as happened when a group of student-prophets saw their ax disappear in the water and Elisha entered the scene and made the object float, so that it could be recovered (2 Kings 6:1-7). And when we are thirsty and look for a place where we can quench our thirst, there is no tap in a place where there was none just minutes before. But that is what happened, we are told, when Hagar was near death in the desert, and when suddenly there was a well that had not been there when she sat down at that spot (Genesis 16:8-21).

The New Testament stories of miracles—mostly performed by Jesus, but also by his disciples/apostles themselves, or also for their benefit when they faced hardships during their missionary work—are better known to many of us than those of the Old Testament. We read about Jesus healing sick men and women from physical and mental ailments, and even bringing a few dead people back to life. And we also encounter stories that tell us how Jesus changed water into wine and fed thousands of people by miraculously multiplying a few loaves of bread and a few fishes. To many ears such stories sound just as improbable as the fourteenth-century story about the bread-turned-stone in Leyden.

Must all these biblical stories really be taken at face value? Including the 'mother-of-all-miracles,' the resurrection of Jesus Christ? Or is there perhaps another way of looking at what happened to Jesus? Must the resurrection perhaps be understood in a spiritual sense? Could it mean that, in spite of the tragic death of their Master, the disciples began to understand the great significance of what he had taught them and the values he represented, and that, as a result, Jesus became alive again, as the Christ, in their hearts?

Am I raising too many questions? By now some readers may want to know more about my own thoughts and are looking for some answers instead of being confronted with ever more questions. Just hold on for a little. I promise I will try to offer some answers as we proceed.

THEOLOGIANS ABOUT GOD

Theologians and Bible scholars are supposed to help us along our pilgrimage of faith. Indeed, many of them see that as their sacred task and have helped numerous men and women deal constructively with their doubts. But some theologians have, in fact, increased the doubts in the minds of many of the people who have listened to them and read their books. There are theologians who deny the possibility of 'revelation' in the classic sense of the word and stress the human element in the origin of the Bible—to the extent that very little of the divine aspect remains. One theologian expressed it in these, frequently quoted, words: 'Everything from above comes from below.'[12] In somewhat more enigmatic words another theologian claimed that 'God is so great that he does not need to exist.'[13] In ordinary languages this means God is a product of our own mind. We create our own concept of God.

For many faithful believers it was, and is, a shock, to hear prominent theologians deny what they have always believed is the core of the Christian faith: God exists and he has revealed himself in the Bible (the written Word) and through Jesus Christ (the living Word). Many believers just shake their heads and simply regard such statements as proof of a satanic infiltration into the church. But many others are profoundly influenced by these ideas and see them, in fact, as confirmation of what they had themselves been thinking all along, but were not able to express so eloquently in words.

We find a reflection of this idea—that everything we say about 'above' must come from below—in the way many postmodern people today think and speak about God. They claim they believe in God, but their concept of God is not only—and sometimes not primarily, or not at all—rooted in the Bible. The biblical God is the kind of God they do not feel attracted to. Their God is often a curious mix of elements they have picked from many different sources—consciously or without realizing it. Their God definitely 'comes from below.'

SO, WHAT TO DO WITH DOUBT?

Doubt is not a recent phenomenon. In a carefully researched, but highly readable, book historian Jennifer Michael Hecht tells the story of doubt as it presented itself through the ages in different forms.[14] She traces the history of doubt from Greek antiquity until 'modern' times. I hope this chapter has given a brief but useful survey of the kind of doubts that exist in our day and age, and the reasons for the doubts of many who are 'on the margins' of the church. I emphasized how today the disturbing *why*-question looms larger in many Christian minds than ever before. Can there be a God who is love, and yet allows so much suffering—if he is also almighty? We focused on the difficulties many have when reading their Bible and when trying to relate their faith to the scientific worldview of our age, and we saw how many are unable to give the miraculous a clear place in their thinking. What do we do with all this doubt?

Before we try to suggest any answers, we must mention yet another kind of doubt. Even if, in spite of our questions and uncertainties, we continue to believe deep down that God does exist and that, in spite of the many problems we recognize, the Bible is a very special book, there remains another area of doubt. This concerns some (or many?) of the doctrines of the church. This is an aspect that is not unique to Seventh-day Adventists, but it may affect—at least so it seems to me—many of my fellow-believers more acutely than the majority of Christians in most other denominations. This is for the simple reason that the Adventist Church insists that, if we want to be 'true' Adventists, we must believe in all its 'fundamental' doctrines. For many this is extremely problematic, as they have come to wonder whether all of these doctrines have a solid biblical basis. To this issue we will now turn in the next chapter.

---

1 I am indebted to Bobby Conway for pointing me to this experience of Steve Jobs in his book *Doubting toward Faith: The Journey to Confident Christianity* (Eugene, OR: Harvest House Publishers, 2015), p. 50. The story is described in Jobs' biography by Walter Isaacson, *Steve Jobs* (New York: Simon & Schuster, 2011), pp. 14, 15.

2 http://www.merriam-webster.com/dictionary.theodicy.

3 Richard Rice, *Suffering and the Search for Meaning: Contemporary Responses to the Problem of Pain* (Downers Grove: IVP Academic Press, 2015).

4 This theory is referred to as 'open theism' or as 'process-theology' (an approach that goes, in fact, beyond 'open theism'). Richard Rice is an important process-theologian.

5 See also my book *Faith: Step by Step: Finding God and Yourself* (Grantham, UK: Stanborough Press, 2006). A few paragraphs from this book have been rephrased in this section.

6 Ellen G. White, *Great Controversy*, pp. v-vii; *Selected Messages,* vol. 1, pp. 16, 19, 20.

7 The minutes of this conference were nowhere to be found until 1975, when the conference transcripts were discovered in the archives of the headquarters of the Adventist Church. Transcript excerpts were first published in 1979 by *Spectrum* magazine and are now available in their entirety on an official church website. For the full reports, see http://docs.adventistarchives.org/documents.asp?CatID=19&SortBy=1&ShowDateOrder=True

8 http://www.evilbible.com/.

9 Bobby Conway, op. cit., p. 72.

10 http://www.brainyquote.com/quotes/authors/r/richard_dawkins.html.

11 Maarten 't Hart, *Magdalena* (Amsterdam: Singel Uitgeverijen, 2015).

12 This is the opinion of the well-known Dutch theologian Harry Kuitert, *Alles behalve kennis* (Baarn, the Netherlands: Ten Have, 2012).

13 See the title of the book by Gerrit Manenschijn: *God is zo groot dat hij niet hoeft te bestaan* (Baarn, the Netherlands: Ten Have, 2002).

14 Jennifer Michael Hecht, *Doubt: A History* (San Francisco: HarperCollins, 2004).

CHAPTER 5

Can I still believe this?

(Let me warn you. This chapter goes into quite a bit of detail—maybe too much for the liking of some readers. I hope you will have the stamina to stay with me, for what follows is important if you want to get the full picture. So, take a deep breath and just plough on. Or, at the very least, scan this chapter. You may find it quite rewarding.)

Denominations differ from each other. They must have something special that sets them apart from other faith communities and the differences can indeed be very significant. Although Protestants and Roman Catholics have much in common, the chasm between their teachings is huge. It is unlikely that attempts to bridge these gaps will be successful any time soon. Moreover, Protestants come in a great variety. Liberal churches are miles away in their theology from conservative faith communities. Denominations that belong to one particular 'family of faith' (like Baptists, Lutherans, Reformed, Methodist, etc.) are, of course, much closer to each other. But also in their case there must be some specific viewpoints in which they differ from each other, for a church that has no distinct doctrines or traditions loses its reason for existence.

Some people are members of a particular denomination mainly because this is where they were brought up. They may, however, not always be able to tell you exactly how their church differs theologically from other denominations in the same 'family of faith.' I have often found this with believers in the various conservative Reformed churches in my own country, the Netherlands. These churches, which all are rooted in Calvinism, have frequently split over theological issues that many of their members did not fully (or not at all) understand. I have met members of church A who, in fact, believe what is a specific tenet of church B, and vice versa.

Many people do not worry too much about theological details; they leave that to their pastors and the professors in their theological seminaries. But others are concerned and have serious questions for which they seek answers. Often they wonder, *Can I still believe what I used to believe?* And, if not, how serious is this? Can I still agree with the things I was taught as I prepared for confirmation or baptism? Or have I moved so far away from what I once affirmed, that I must ask myself whether I can still conscientiously stay with my church? Doubts about certain doctrines have pushed these people to 'the margins' of their church. It may be the result of a slow, gradual process. Or the doubts may have been dormant for a long time and then suddenly receive momentum as the result of some personal crisis, or the reading of a particular book or listening to a talk or a sermon.

Some people are actually told by church officials or church boards that they can no longer be members of their church, since they have 'apostatized' from 'the truth.' This happens more often in sect-like movements, or in very strict and conservative denominations, than in the 'main line' churches. These tend to be more accommodating to diversity in opinion. In fact, they have often developed different 'modalities' to make room for those on 'the right on 'the left' and in 'the middle.' This has, in particular, been true of the so-called 'state churches' in Europe that aspired to be a spiritual home for all the people of the entire nation. (In the United States these different streams have tended to organize themselves as separate denominations.)

Thus far, disfellowshipping members for doctrinal reasons is not (or no longer) very common in the Adventist Church, especially not in the Western world. Even when 'heretical' theology teachers were sacked or were forced to resign, they usually did not automatically lose their church membership. Whether one laments or welcomes it, there is actually a substantial diversity of theological standpoints within the Adventist Church. Like many other denominations, Adventism has seen a gradual evolvement of different 'modalities' or streams. It is difficult to define these different streams precisely, even though some have tried to do so. David Newman, a former *Ministry* editor, once suggested that there are at least four distinct streams in Adventism: Mainstream Adventism, Evangelical Adventism, Progressive Adventism and Historic Adventism.[1] A number of years ago I did some *googling* and happened to land on a website that distinguishes no fewer than eight currents in Adventist theology, and gives a few names of key representatives of each of these streams: liberal, progressive, supporters of the moral influence theory, evangelical, moderate, conservative/traditional, ultra-conservative and extreme-ultra conservative.[2] The author has preferred to remain anonymous, but is clearly rather knowledgeable about Adventism. I must admit that I felt good to see my name listed among the six or seven 'progressive' theologians! Nonetheless, I would perhaps draw the lines between the various groups somewhat differently. I do not, for instance, regard the last group of the 'extreme-ultra-conservatives' as a bona fide branch of Adventism. However, the message of the article on this website is clear: *Contemporary Adventism has many different faces.*

The fact that there exists a wide divergence of theological opinion does not mean, however, that there is also great tolerance everywhere and that open and free discussion reigns. Many voices, especially on the conservative side of the church, want to 'clean up' what they feel is a most regrettable situation. They would rather belong to a doctrinally pure church than to a church where one can adjust one's own personal confession of faith! And the recent strong push for a tighter wording of the twenty-eight *Fundamental Beliefs*, with the constant emphasis by key leaders on the fact that adherence to all of these 'fundamentals' is required if one wants to be counted as a genuine Adventist, worries a lot of church members who want more personal freedom in defining what they believe. Also, the attempts of the church's administration to have better control of the orthodoxy of theology teachers in the denominational institutions of higher learning is seen by many as a threat to academic freedom and as an attempt to enforce one particular way of reading the Bible and of 'doing' theology.

In this connection the concept of the 'shaking' is referred to with increasing (and disturbing) frequency. This is the idea that there is a continuous 'sifting' in the church—a process whereby those who were never fully committed to 'the truth' are removed from the church. This process, it is usually suggested, will reach its climax just before the end of time. The 'shaking,' which inevitably results in a large-scale exodus from the church, may therefore, it is suggested or implied by those who speak about this, actually be something positive. For it means that Christ's coming is now nearer than ever![3]

LEAVING VOLUNTARILY

Some believers have struggled with their doctrinal doubts for years, and have at last decided that they cannot in good conscience remain members of their church. Some leave their faith community and do not connect elsewhere. They leave, sometimes without leaving a trace, while others continue to have some—mainly social—ties with their former fellow-believers. Some move to a new spiritual home that accords better with where they presently are in their spiritual pilgrimage. They have decided to say farewell to their former church, sometimes with a sigh of relief, but often with a lot of pain in their hearts.

The Roman Catholic Church loses millions of its members worldwide, who no longer agree with some of the moral obligations the church imposes on them. They protest against the official stance on birth control practices and disagree with the church's absolute refusal to permit same-sex relations between people who want to live in an exclusive, monogamous and permanent relationship. They consider the 'laws' that the clergy must remain celibate and that women cannot become priests as totally outdated and as contrary to the gospel of Jesus Christ.

In strict Calvinist circles many have serious doubts about the gospel basis for the doctrine of predestination. They may have grown up with the doctrine of 'double-predestination.' The argument for this doctrine runs like this: God in his eternal wisdom and in his inscrutable sovereignty decided, before we were even born, whether we will ultimately receive eternal life or will face eternal damnation.

There is nothing we can do about it. Of course, we are expected to live a Christian life and to attend to all our religious duties, but it is fully up to God whether we will 'make it' or not. And if we don't, we have no valid reason to complain! For no human being is entitled to salvation. It is only by his sovereign grace that God elects some to inherit eternity. For many this is an unbearable kind of faith. It means we can only *hope* to be among the elect, but can never be *sure!* Small wonder that many will at some point begin to doubt whether this doctrine agrees with the gospel of Christ, who declared that God 'so loved the world' with the intention that all people would be saved! Some of these doubters will leave their church and say farewell to any form of Christian faith, while others, fortunately, will find another spiritual home where they can experience the assurance of salvation.

The Mormon Church—or the Church of Jesus Christ of Latter-day Saints—is the fourth largest denomination in the United States. This 'American' religion has attracted millions of men and women, and is still able to inspire thousands of young people to commit a year of their life to 'missionary' work in some other part of the world. But the church also sees considerable numbers disappear—for many of the same reasons as we mentioned earlier with regard to Christian churches in general. In addition, the serious gender imbalance in the Mormon Church appears to be a major issue and is reported by researchers as a major cause of leaving the church. But 'apostasy' rates are also significant—even though the church does not publish any statistical data about this. Among the doctrines many ex-Mormons have mentioned as reasons for their increasing doubts about the truth of their religion are the importance that is attached to other books (the *Book of Mormon,* the *Book of the Covenant* and the *Pearl of Great Price*) besides the Bible, the practice of baptizing on behalf of deceased people, and various secret rituals.

We could mention a long list of specific doctrinal views that cause much discussion or dissent in other denominations. But our focus is on the Seventh-day Adventist Church and in the following pages I will review some of the issues that seem to surface most frequently when Adventists speak of their doubts regarding certain teachings of their church. I am not listing them in any specific order, since I am not aware of any study that indicates which of those points rank highest as reasons of doubt.

INSPIRATION

I want to add just a little more to what I have already said about the Adventist doctrine of inspiration. It is a key issue, for our view of the inspiration and the transmission of the Bible determines whether we opt for a 'plain' reading of the Bible (that takes what we read as literally as possible), or whether we allow a greater role for the human instruments that God used in communicating with us.

There is good reason to expect that in the near future the topics of inspiration and hermeneutics (how to interpret the Bible) will receive increased attention from the leadership of the Adventist Church and will in the coming years demand a significant portion of the time and energy of the personnel of the *Biblical Research Institute* (BRI) at the denominational headquarters. A number of relatively recent publications of the BRI go a long way towards supporting a 'plain' reading approach.[4]

It is noteworthy to see that recently number one of the *Fundamental Beliefs* has been somewhat 'tightened.' This article of 'the twenty-eight' tells us that the Scriptures are 'the infallible revelation of God's will.' But it also stresses that these writings are the 'authoritative revealer of doctrines and the trustworthy record of God's acts in history.' Much depends on the way the terms 'infallible,' 'authoritative' and 'trustworthy' are defined. In the recent update of 'the twenty-eight' we now read that the Bible is not only 'authoritative' and 'infallible,' but also *'final,'* and that it is the *'definitive'* revealer of doctrines. The new formulation of *Fundamental Belief* number ten also confirms that the *Fundamental Beliefs* advocate a very narrow view of inspiration.

The most authoritative document about the Adventist approach to the Bible and its interpretation, to date, besides the formulation in the *Fundamental Beliefs,* is the so-called *Rio Document.* This was the outcome of a study process in the 1980s, which culminated in a formal declaration that was accepted by the executive committee of the General Conference during its 'autumn council' in 1996.[5] This document rejects the quite commonly held scholarly view that many of the biblical writings have gone through a long process of collection and 'redaction' before they attained the form that became the basis for our modern translations. The majority of biblical scholars have, for instance, concluded that the five books of Moses consist of several documents that originated in different circles, were written at different times, and were only later brought together in the so-called Pentateuch (the five scrolls). Or, to take another example of this approach that is usually referred to as the 'historical-critical method': the majority of Old Testament experts believe that the book of Isaiah had two, or perhaps three, different authors. The *Rio Document* does not want to hear of this. (Strangely enough, Adventist biblical scholars seem to have much less hesitation in identifying different sources for the four gospels![6]) Adventist scholarly opinion is starkly divided about this issue. Those who belong to the *Adventist Theological Society*[7] support the position that is outlined in the *Rio Document*. In fact, one cannot become a member of this influential theological society, without signing a written declaration that one agrees with this particular view of the inspiration and transmission of the Bible.

It is clear that one's view of the origin and nature of the Bible also determines to a major extent how one approaches individual doctrines and ethical issues, such as creation and women's ordination. Likewise it is important for one's view of the ministry and the writings of Ellen G. White (see below).

When church members begin to entertain doubts about the approach to inspiration that is currently strongly promoted by the leadership of the church, and by organizations that support this position, it is frequently the starting point for doubts in other doctrinal areas. Many of these doubters will less and less appreciate denominational publications and other church media products that espouse the 'plain reading' approach. Many will look for spiritual nurture from other sources, but exposure to these may, in fact, raise new questions in their minds regarding certain traditional Adventist teachings.

THE TRINITY

Doubt about the doctrine of the Trinity is not something that has recently surfaced in Adventist circles. In fact, for a considerable time, many Adventists (including some of the early leaders) were solid anti-Trinitarians, that is, they did not believe in the doctrine of the Trinity. Uriah Smith, the well-known pioneer and the author of books on Daniel and the Revelation, commented, for instance, on the text in Revelation which calls Christ 'the Alpha and the Omega' (1:9). He argued that, while Christ already existed long before the creation of the world, he was not from all eternity, like the Father. Christ had a beginning somewhere in the distant past. With other Adventist pioneers, as e.g. James White, who had also come from the Christian Connection,[8] Smith believed that the Son is subordinate to God the Father, and that the idea of a Trinity of three eternal, fully equal beings is not biblical. Ellen White never spoke in anti-Trinitarian terms, but it is was not until later in life that she clearly stated her support for the view of a Trinity—Father, Son and Spirit as co-eternal, fully equal beings. However, interestingly enough she never actually used the term Trinity!

It was not until well into the twentieth century that the Adventist Church officially declared itself to be fully in the Trinitarian camp, even though there continued to be dissenting voices. But more recently, those who doubt or reject a Trinitarian theology seem to be on the increase.[9] And although many on the 'left' side of the church have questions or even doubts about this key Christian doctrine, the most vocal voices opposing this doctrine tend to be on the 'right' side of the theological spectrum. There are conservative Adventists who believe that the Trinity doctrine is, in fact, a Roman Catholic (and therefore, by definition, false!) teaching, and that Adventism must be wary of drifting towards Roman Catholicism, and should return to the historical (non-Trinitarian) faith of its pioneers.

Even though the doctrine of the Trinity is a cornerstone of Christian theology, (strangely enough) in Adventist circles doubt about this pivotal doctrine is generally considered much less serious than, for instance, questioning a literal six-day creation or a literal interpretation of the heavenly sanctuary. My credentials as a pastor would be at greater risk if I were to light a cigarette publicly than if I were to express doubt about the Trinity doctrine in a sermon. Uncertainty about this important doctrine does not weigh as heavily on the hearts of most Adventist leaders as uncertainty about a few other doctrines that we will now briefly discuss.

THE HUMAN NATURE OF CHRIST

Was Christ divine and human at the same time? If so, how can that be? And how must we understand the humanness of Christ? Was he exactly like us, or not quite? The early church needed centuries of study and vigorous debate before its leaders, meeting in councils in Nicea (325 AD), Chalcedon (451 AD) and other places, arrived at detailed formulas about the two natures of Christ which were satisfactory to the majority of Christian believers. But ever since the Christian church has officially confessed that Christ is 'very God' and simultaneously 'very man.'

Most early Adventists did not worry too much about the mystery of the natures of Christ. Their focus was on the current status and role of Jesus Christ. They believed that he ascended to heaven as our 'high priest,' and that since 1844 he has been involved in a heavenly activity that was prefigured in the Old Testament sanctuary service as the 'Day of Atonement.' But as time passed the issue of the two natures of Christ began to demand more attention. Especially since the publication of the book *Seventh-day Adventists Answer Questions on Doctrine*[10] the issue has become rather controversial, as that book defined the human nature of Christ in a way that was, and is, unacceptable to many.

In essence, there are three competing views about the human nature of Christ.
1. Christ was in everything exactly like us. He shared the same human weaknesses and experienced the same propensity (inclination) toward sin with all human beings;
2. Christ was fully man in the sense that he took the kind of human nature that Adam had before the fall; and

3. Christ inherited our human nature but without the inherited bent towards sin that we must contend with. However, this 'advantage' was more than offset by the fact that Christ was infinitely more severely tempted than we will ever be.

Which of these views has the strongest biblical credentials? Here opinions differ sharply. Running to Ellen G. White for a clear-cut answer does not really help, for her many statements about the nature of Christ point us in different directions, and through a selective consultation of her writings one can find support for each of these viewpoints.[11]

Many church members will shrug their shoulders and say, 'What is all the fuss about? Is it really important? Surely, we can never hope to understand how one Person can be divine and human at the same time. Therefore, let us not rack our brains over this mystery.' However, the issue is more important than it may seem on the surface, and there are some major ramifications that cause many 'believers on the margins' to be unhappy with their church. Let me explain.

First of all, we should look at article number four of the *Fundamental Beliefs:*

'Forever *truly God,* He [Christ] became also *truly human,* Jesus the Christ. He was conceived of the Holy Spirit and born of the virgin Mary. He lived and *experienced temptation as a human being,* but *perfectly exemplified the righteousness and love of God.* By his miracles he manifested God's power and was attested as God's promised Messiah. He suffered and died voluntarily on the cross for our sins and in our place, was raised from the dead, and ascended to heaven to minister in the heavenly sanctuary on our behalf. He will come again in glory for the final deliverance of his people and the restoration of all things' (italics added).

A few important elements are emphasized: (1) Christ's full divinity; (2) the virgin birth; (3) Christ's full humanity; and (4) the fact that he could serve as a perfect role model for us. We are told in this article that Christ was 'human,' but the formulation judiciously avoids any precise definition of that term. Personally, I would be quite happy to leave it at that. For how can we ever define something that is totally unique? We have nothing to compare it with. However, not everybody is prepared to simply accept and live with this strange paradox of full divinity and full humanity in one Person.

What is the wider issue? It is argued that if Christ took the kind of human nature that Adam had *before* he 'fell' into sin, he ceases to be our perfect example. For if this were so, he had a distinct advantage over us and, therefore, we are not to be blamed if we cannot live up to the standard he has set before us. On the other hand, if Christ took the kind of human nature that Adam had *after* the 'fall,' and was nonetheless able to remain sinless, it is, in principle, also possible for us to arrive at a point in our lives where we can live without sin. In other words, *perfection is possible*—not just in the world to come, but already here, on this earth—if we fully commit ourselves to Christ and are determined to overcome all our wrongdoings and to live in daily harmony with the will of God.

Few people, if any, in the Adventist Church would deny that God wants us to grow spiritually and to model our lives after our great Example, Jesus Christ. But a large percentage of church members would also recognize (I hope and think) that they are sinners and that they are far from perfect, and will never be fully sinless until the moment they are recreated as perfect beings in a world made new. They believe that the Bible is clear on this point: Nobody is without sin. Anyone who claims to be sinless is a 'liar' (1 John 1:8).

Without getting into a lot of theological technicalities, I believe it would be fair to say that the idea that perfection is within human reach has led many on the dangerous path of legalism. This has always been a trap for conservative Christians, and, in particular, for Seventh-day Adventists. Salvation is by faith in Jesus Christ and not by what we do ourselves. But for those who stress the eternal validity of the law of God, trying to score brownie points with God through a meticulous obedience to his law has always represented a major temptation. Therefore, the assumption that we can live perfectly, because Christ was perfect and was in all things completely the same as we are, can easily lead to a very legalistic approach to religion, in which much of the joy of the gospel falls by the wayside. And there is the perception (whether fully justified or not) on the part of the believers who are 'on the margins' of the church, that those who strive towards perfection are not always the most pleasant people to associate with. When these 'perfectionists' are able to set the tone in a local church, many of those who are 'on the margins' feel suffocated and unable to breath in the (often legalistic) environment they stimulate. Many of them will eventually give up and leave.

The idea that perfection is possible has further ramifications and is closely connected to what is commonly referred to as the 'last-generation-theology' (*LGT*). Supporters of this view combine a number of elements from the Adventist tradition: the 'great controversy' concept, the theme of the 'remnant,' the possibility of perfection, and the role of Christ in the heavenly sanctuary.

Let me try to summarize this *LGT* (last-generation-theology) in a few words: Before Christ's second coming the true believers, who 'keep all God's commandments' (including the seventh-day Sabbath) and who have 'the testimony of Jesus' (identified as the 'spirit of prophecy'= Mrs Ellen G. White), will form a relatively small 'remnant.' They will come to the point that they have overcome all sin and have reached a state of full perfection. This is essential, for 'probation' closes when Christ has finished his intercessory work in the heavenly sanctuary. In the very final period of this earth's history—before Christ appears— those who belong to the remnant must be perfect since they will have to live for some time without an Intercessor.

This may be a somewhat simplified version of the 'last-generation-theology,' but it captures the essence. The main architect of this 'theology' was M.L. Andreasen (1876-1962), who was a prominent Adventist theologian but later fell from denominational grace, and even lost his credentials for a period of time shortly before his death. There have been periods in the past when this 'theology' was very influential, for instance during the time when Robert Pierson was president of the Adventist Church (1966-1979). It has made a very strong comeback in recent times and finds a strong supporter in Ted N.C. Wilson, the current president of the Adventist denomination.

For many 'believers on the margins' all of this feels rather uneasy and seems to have a totally different ring to it than the joyful, straightforward message of the gospel of salvation and of freedom in Jesus Christ. They may not know all the details of the arguments that are put forward to defend this particular view of the human nature of Christ, the emphasis on perfectionism and this last-generation-theology, but they see how it affects many of its proponents and how it often feeds an intolerant attitude towards those with other views. They may not understand all the reasoning behind it, and may not have read any books about it or studied and compared all the relevant Ellen G. White statements. And doubt may perhaps not be the best description of their feelings towards this type of Adventism, but they have this mostly intuitive sense that this is not their 'cup of tea.' This type of 'theology' does not produce the kind of religious experience that nurtures their faith and makes them happy people. Having too much of this around them makes them want to escape.

THE SANCTUARY

It is often claimed that the sanctuary doctrine is the only teaching that is truly unique to Adventism. Losing this element of the Adventist heritage is, therefore, said to endanger the very reason for the existence of the Adventist Church as a distinct denomination. There are other groups of Christians who keep the Sabbath on the seventh day of the week and many Christians proclaim the soon coming of Christ, but there are no exact parallels to the Adventist view of the sanctuary. However, the sanctuary doctrine is not only unique, it is also the most *controversial,* and has been attacked and criticized by many outside Adventism as well as by many church members. One can trace a constant history of doubt about, and resistance to, this doctrine as it is traditionally formulated.

In Old Testament times God instituted a *tableau vivant* (dramatic representation) to impress upon the Israelite people that the rupture between him and mankind could only be breached by a gracious divine intervention. This intervention was very expensive; it required a costly sacrifice. An elaborate system of sacrifices was given to the people, to get the message across that all of this pointed to the ultimate Sacrifice, which would restore the relationship between man and God. Christ was that Sacrifice, but was also symbolized by the priests, and in particular the high priest, who prefigured the role of Christ as the great High Priest, as is described in the Letter to the Hebrews. Thus, everything that happened in the Old Testament sanctuary service, all the different services—daily and annually—and all those who served in the sanctuary were a collective symbol of Jesus Christ and his saving work.

On the basis of several prophetic statements in the Bible, William Miller developed a theory that Christ's return was imminent and could be expected 'around 1843.' Later he became more specific and, finally, agreed with some of the other Millerite preachers that the Second Coming would take place on October 22, 1844. This fateful day, however, became the day of the 'great disappointment' for the Millerite believers, when it passed without any sign of Christ's coming.

In the days and weeks after this disheartening experience the disillusioned Adventist believers wondered what had gone wrong. Had there been a mistake in their calculations? Or had the calculations been correct, but had they been mistaken in the event that would occur on that day? A group of these Advent-believers soon concluded that on this date—22 October 1844—Christ had begun his service as the heavenly High Priest in the sanctuary in heaven. This was his special work that was prefigured by the elaborate ritual on the Day of Atonement in Israel's sanctuary service. It was further argued that the annual Day of Atonement was, in a sense, a kind of judgment day. The sins that the people had confessed during the year, and for which they had brought their sacrificial offerings throughout the year, were blotted out on the 'Yom Kippur'—the Day of Atonement. This annual service pointed forward to the work of Christ in heaven, during the so-called 'investigative' or 'pre-Advent' phase of the judgment, in which it was to become clear who will be saved and who will be lost.

Where are the problems for many of those who are 'on the margins'? In the past the doubts centered, in particular, on two issues. Firstly, it concerned the question whether the work of Christ was really finished on the cross or whether the atonement was incomplete until Christ had performed his high priestly work in the heavenly sanctuary. For many it was (and is) important to emphasize that Christ's sacrifice on the cross was final and that his atoning work should not be split into a first and a second phase, as the traditional Adventist sanctuary doctrine seems to do.

And, secondly, there was the role of Azazel. If you are not sure what or who Azazel is, you may want to read up on the Old Testament Day of Atonement ritual in Leviticus 16. At the end of the ceremonies of that day a male goat was sent into the desert, carrying away all the sins of the people (verse 16). According to the traditional Adventist explanation, every detail of the Old Testament ritual has a counterpart in the 'real' Day of Atonement' in which Christ officiates. The male goat, called Azazel, is understood as a symbol of the Satan. There was fierce protest against this view, since this seems to imply that Adventists actually believe that Satan plays a role in our redemption from sin.

Of late, the objections of many 'sanctuary-doubters' (at least those that I hear) tend to be more general and/or focus on other aspects. The objectors find it difficult to accept the idea that there must be some sort of literal, material, edifice in heaven, with literal furniture and artifacts, and with two separate apartments, as many of their fellow-Adventists claim. They find it quite ridiculous to believe that in October 1844 Jesus Christ walked from one apartment in this heavenly location to the next, where he has remained ever since, working hard to ensure that no mistakes will be made in the heavenly accounting of human sin. Must we really believe in such a literal application of the Old Testament symbolism, they wonder?

A probably even more fundamental objection is the fact that the traditional Adventist sanctuary doctrine does not start with the New Testament description of the heavenly sanctuary service, as found in the Letter to the Hebrews, but with the Old Testament account of the

Day of Atonement. Rather than interpreting the Old Testament ritual in the light of the commentary given in the New Testament, this later (inspired) interpretation is forced into the Old Testament mode.

1844

For many the 1844 date is a sacred aspect of Adventist teaching. Older Adventists will remember the schematic representations of the '2300 evenings and mornings,' with the 457 BC date at one end and 1844 at the other end, and somewhere in the middle the symbol of the cross. Today, even most Adventists who insist on the importance of the 1844 date would not be able to explain how this date of October 1844 is arrived at. And, indeed, it requires some complex reasoning. The doubters would say that it also takes a series of assumptions that they see as extremely shaky.

Traditional Adventist teaching maintains that we find a time prophecy in the book of Daniel that brings us to the year 1844, as the moment when something significant happened in heaven. To arrive at this conclusion, one must be willing to take a series of steps. In the first place, one must accept that the book Daniel was written by a prophet who lived and worked at the Babylonian court, and later at the Persian court, in the sixth century BC, and that he conveyed a number of prophetic messages that relate to the period from his days until the end of time. Today most experts on the book of Daniel believe that this section of the Bible was actually written in the second century BC, by an unknown author who used the name of the prophet Daniel to give his document more authority. Nowadays this procedure would be considered extremely deceitful, but in ancient times this was a rather common practice. In the standard Adventist interpretation of the book the evil power that plays a key role ('the little horn') refers to the Roman Catholic Church. Most scholars today argue that this 'little horn' is a symbol for a Greek king, Antiochus IV Epiphanes, who gave the Jewish people a hard time and desecrated the Jerusalem temple in 168 BC.

To arrive at the traditional Adventist view regarding the time prophecy of the 2,300 days as ending in 1844, one must go against majority scholarly opinion and stick to the early (sixth century BC) date of the book and reject the alternative theory that many find far more convincing. It should be said, however, that there are also some good arguments for an early dating of the book. Nevertheless, it is good to know that approaches to the book of Daniel differ sharply.

The next step to arrive at the 1844 date would be to accept that Daniel 8, in which the time period of 2,300 days is mentioned, is connected with Daniel 9, where the starting point of this prophetic period is allegedly found. Daniel did not understand the vision of chapter 8 about the 2,300 days and kept worrying about its possible meaning. In Daniel 9, so the explanation runs, he is given the key. A new time period is mentioned: seventy weeks are 'cut off' for a specific purpose. It is argued that the period of the seventy weeks is, in fact, the first section of the 2,300 days. Thus, if we know the starting point of the seventy-week period of Daniel 9, we also know when the 2,300 days of Daniel 8 began. The problem that many interpreters, however, see is that there is a considerable lapse of time (some twelve years) between Daniel's vision in chapter 8 and the one in Daniel 9, which makes this connection not as probable, they say, as Adventists have traditionally argued.

But then there is the next hurdle. In Adventist teaching the starting point for the seventy weeks, and therefore presumably also for the 2,300 days, is found in Daniel 9:25. It is, we read in this text, the moment when a ruler would issue a decree that would allow the Judeans, who had been living as exiles in Babylon, to return to Palestine and to rebuild Jerusalem. The traditional interpretation tells us that this decree was issued by the Persian king Artaxerxes I in 457 BC. However, more than one such decree was issued and not all would agree that this particular decree of Artaxerxes is the one Daniel 9:25 refers to, and that we can therefore safely pick the 457 BC date as the beginning of the seventy weeks and of the 2,300 days.

This does not exhaust the number of steps we must take to eventually get to 1844. A key assumption is that in biblical time prophecies a *prophetic day* must be interpreted as a *literal year.* If this is true, and if the choice of the 457 BC date is correct, and if the periods in Daniel 8 and 9 do run concurrently, then, indeed 2,300 prophetic days are

2,300 literal years and reach as far as 1844. But is there a solid basis for this so-called 'day-year principle'?

The 'day-year principle' is not an Adventist invention, but has been used by many expositors of prophecy in the past. However, this was in a time when the majority of these expositors saw the 'apocalyptic' prophecies (especially in the Bible books of Daniel and the Revelation) as a description of the history of the world until the second coming of Christ. Today most Bible scholars prefer other approaches to these prophetic portions of the Bible, and few would still defend the 'day-year-principle.' They point out that the two texts that are usually cited in defense of this principle (Numbers 14:34 and Ezekiel 4:5-6) are not very conclusive—certainly not when read in their contexts.

Another question regarding the October 22, 1844 date, that remains rather puzzling to most Adventists (and not just to those 'on the margins'), is that a special kind of Jewish calendar is used to determine on what day the tenth day of the Jewish month Tishri (on which the Jewish Day of Atonement was to be celebrated) fell in that year. The Adventist 'pioneers' who developed the sanctuary doctrine opted for the calendar of the Jewish Karaite movement. For most church members who try to understand the basis for the sanctuary doctrine, it remains a mystery why they preferred this particular calendar.

Yet other issues emerge. In the *King James Version* Daniel 8:14 reads as follows: 'Unto two thousand and three hundred days; then shall the sanctuary be *cleansed*.' Other versions indicate that the sanctuary was to be *restored,* or 'to be *restored in its rightful state.* The entire doctrine stands or falls with the identification of the sanctuary and the interpretation of the term 'cleansing' or 'restoring.' For traditional Adventism, which places Daniel in the sixth century BC, it is clear that the sanctuary that is to be 'cleansed' must refer to the heavenly sanctuary, as the Jerusalem temple no longer existed at the end of the 2,300 *year* period.

Many Adventists 'on the margins' wonder how anything so complicated as the traditional Adventist sanctuary doctrine can be crucial to our faith. They believe that Christ is their Mediator and that because of him they can feel secure. But this idea of a literal sanctuary in heaven, where Christ entered in 1844 for a final phase in his redemptive work, does not sound very convincing to them. And how relevant can it be to tell others about something that supposedly happened in 1844? Is it not far more important to worry about the significance of the gospel message in the first part of the twenty-first century?

It should be added that doubt about the traditional sanctuary doctrine is not limited to 'believers on the margins.'[12] Both anecdotal evidence and some firmer data suggest that many church members have deep misgivings about the traditional sanctuary views, and especially about the interpretation of Daniel 8:14 and the arithmetic that is based on this text.[13] There is also more than just anecdotal evidence to indicate that a significant percentage of Adventist pastors no longer supports the traditional view.[14]

END TIME PROPHECIES

Another area that is a major source of unease and doubt among Adventist 'believers on the margins' is the traditional approach to the prophecies of Daniel and the Revelation in general. Although the details of the traditional interpretation of these prophetic books are not spelled out in the *Fundamental Beliefs*, voicing doubts about these is extremely upsetting to many who maintain that Adventism loses its identity if we no longer preach and believe the 'Truth' as it was explained in the classic tomes the Adventists pioneers wrote, or—at the very least—is presented in a somewhat updated version by current publications from our official publishing houses and (even more so) by independent publishers on the 'right' side of the church. I personally experienced the displeasure of the *Biblical Research Institute* of the General Conference (and of a number of church leaders), when I wrote my PhD dissertation about Adventist attitudes towards Roman Catholicism and pleaded for a critical revision of some of our traditional views.[15]

According to the Adventist interpretation of Daniel and the Revelation these portions of Scripture tell us about 'the great controversy' between good and evil through the ages. The symbols are applied to historical events and to specific political and spiritual *powers,* and at times also to clearly identifiable *persons* of the past, the present and the future. The apostasy in the Christian Church is said to have culminated in the papal church, which persecuted God's people in the past and will do so again with even greater vengeance in the future—with the assistance of 'apostate' Protestantism and various occult powers. Everything moves inexorably towards a grim climax, just before the second coming of Christ, when a small remnant of those who have remained loyal will have to face relentless opposition from all God's enemies, who together form the 'spiritual Babylon.'

The remnant is—according to this view—the Seventh-day-Adventist Church, or the core of Adventist believers who have remained loyal to the truth of the 'three angels' messages.' In the final conflict the Sabbath will play an ever more crucial role. Sunday-keepers will be recognized by the 'mark of the beast,' while the Sabbath-keepers carry the 'seal' of God! Sunday laws will be proclaimed in a worldwide, deadly campaign against God's remnant, in which Roman Catholicism, with the support of Protestantism, will join forces with the United States of America.

Admittedly, most Adventists who hold these views will not brand all non-Adventists as 'Babylon' and will not condemn all fellow-Christians who try to serve their God to the best of their knowledge. It is clear, however, that this overall Adventist prophetic scenario does not encourage any close ties with other Christian communities or inter-church cooperation. All positive signals from ecumenical organizations towards the Adventist Church tend to be viewed with deep suspicion, since we (we think) know where it will ultimately lead.

It is an understatement to say that many 'believers on the margins' are no longer at ease with this general scenario. They wonder how many of the historic applications that have been made are truly valid. They know that many interpretations have had to be modified as events did not actually pan out in ways that were expected. They wonder whether Catholics are our enemies and whether other

Christians deserve our distrust. And they ask, Is the Catholic Church of Pope Francis the same as the medieval institution that sponsored the Inquisition? Do not all Christians in today's world face common challenges? Is the rampant secularism of our times not a far greater danger than the forms of Christianity that differ from Adventism? Is the growth of the Islamic religion, even in the West, not a much bigger headache than an ecumenical movement that may have some aspects we do not like?

Even if one agrees that Adventism may rightfully claim that it must bring a special message which emphasizes aspects of the gospel that are mostly neglected by others—does that warrant the belief that only Adventist believers constitute the 'remnant' church, and therefore is the only community of believers that is going to 'make' it in the end? For 'believers on the margins' the traditional Adventist prophetic views represent more and more an area of doubt. They ask themselves, Do I want to live in this atmosphere where I must assume that I am the only one who is right and that all others are wrong? Should I not rather focus on Christ as my Friend than on other Christians as my enemies?

ELLEN G. WHITE

Few Adventists, if any, will deny that Mrs Ellen G. White has played an important role in the Seventh-day Adventist Church. She is nowadays often—and correctly so—referred to as one of the co-founders of the Adventist Church. Most Adventists will also agree that she was an extraordinary woman, who in spite of a very limited formal education had a major influence on the thinking of early Adventism and on the development of the church's philosophy in such areas as education, health, and evangelism. Opinions begin to differ when her capacities and accomplishments are described as the result of a prophetic gift, and when she is elevated to the status of a prophet.

Much, of course, depends on how the term 'prophet' is defined. Was she a person who was used by God in the early phase of the Adventist Church, like, for instance Martin Luther at the time of the sixteenth-century Reformation, or John Wesley in the formative phase of

Methodism? Or was she a prophet who was inspired in the sense that everything she wrote should, in every detail, be applied to us who live and 'do' church under totally different circumstances? Should we also opt for a 'plain reading' method with regard to the writings of Ellen White? And is what she said and wrote the final word about the interpretation of the Bible and the definitive criterion for determining correct doctrines?

While official Adventist teaching is clear that the Ellen G. White writings do not possess the same authority as the Bible, many Adventists 'on the margins' are disturbed by the undeniable fact that, in actual practice, Ellen White is often not held against the light of the Scriptures, but that it is frequently rather the other way around. Many seem to use Ellen G. White as the infallible guide to the correct meaning and application of the Bible. Moreover, her words are often applied to today's situations, without any regard for the totally different context in which she lived and worked. Many of those who are 'on the margins' are upset when a sermon (as often happens) contains more Ellen White quotations than Bible references and when the mantra of 'Ellen White says,' or simply 'she says,' is invoked to settle everything.

It must be admitted that among the critics of Ellen G. White are many who have never read any of her books, and who know very little about her important role in early Adventist history. Yet it would be too easy to say that any doubts about the ministry of Ellen White will quickly disappear if people would simply read more of what she has written. There are many who have (more or less successfully) tried to peruse such books as *Patriarchs and Prophets*, *The Desire of Ages* and *The Great Controversy*, and have found lots of uplifting and inspiring thoughts. But they are not necessarily convinced that everything Mrs White wrote is historically fully correct, and that the way in which she understood biblical and historical events is the only possible perspective. Moreover, they have also read *about* Ellen White and have discovered that Ellen White did not always claim for herself what many of her admirers claim for her. And, to their dismay, they found that she often 'borrowed' heavily from others. They discovered that

Ellen White was an ordinary, far from perfect, human being, who was not always consistent, could change her mind and sometimes times modified her thinking over the years.

Many Adventists 'on the margins' protest against the way in which Ellen White is put on a pedestal and is made into the final arbiter for everything. They dislike this trend in their local church, when Ellen White is treated as a saint and is used as an instrument to criticize those who may have other opinions regarding issue of theology and life-style. And they similarly have an aversion when top church leaders use her words—often totally out of context—to solve every problem and answer every question. In fact, many 'believers on the margins' feel that the way in which Ellen G. White and the 'Spirit of Prophecy' are *used* (the choice of that verb is intentional) risks making the Adventist Church into a religious sect.

LIFE STYLE ISSUES

In addition to the doctrines that cause many church members to wonder, 'Can I still believe this?' other oft-heard doubts have to do with life-style issues. How biblical are the Adventist 'rules' about food, jewelry, recreation, cohabitation and sex (including same-sex relationships)? Are some of these restrictions not simply the residue of a Victorian heritage? Are most of them not primarily 'Ellen-White-based' rather than Bible-based? Do at least some of these prohibitions not conflict with the gospel principle of freedom in Christ?

At this point I simply want to mention this area of concern. And let me just say that, in all honesty, doubts in this category may (at least to some extent and in some cases) reflect a desire to justify one's own behavior and are often not really a thoroughly considered, theologically rooted doubt.

More could have been said about doubts regarding particular doctrines and about the important question whether a church organization may demand allegiance to such an extended array of doctrinal positions, without allowing considerable diversity of opinion, and without calling for tolerance towards each other when people think differently. Many struggle with the dilemma of what they must do with their doubts and with opinions that differ from the official church standard as codified in the twenty-eight *Fundamental Beliefs*. Can they still claim to be 'real' Adventists? Can they in good conscience remain Adventist Church members? Must they remain 'on the margins'? Can they rediscover a satisfying role for themselves in the Adventist Church? Or is there no other way out of this dilemma than a complete exit from the Adventist community?

In the next chapter I want to return to the topic of doubt in general: doubt about God and doubt about the church. In a later chapter we will focus on dealing with doubts with regard to specific doctrines. I will not have answers to every question. I am myself constantly confronted with doubts and questions—about my faith, my church, and important facets of Adventist beliefs. But I hope that what follows will help the readers of this book to find some 'handles' to deal meaningfully with their questions and doubts.

---

1 See 'How Much Diversity Can We Stand?' in Ministry (April 1994), pp. 5, 27; See also William G. Johnsson, *The Fragmenting of Adventism* (Boise, ID: Pacific Press, 1995), pp. 91-95. A. LeRoy Moore, *Adventism: Resolving Issues that Divide Us* (Hagerstown, MD: Review and Herald, 1995) focuses on the divergence in views regarding law and grace, the atonement and the natures of Christ.

2 http://christianforums.com/member.php?u=185580.

3 Roger W. Coon, 'Shaking,' in: Denis Fortin and Jerry Moon, eds., *The Ellen G. White Encyclopedia* (Hagerstown: Review and Herald, 2013), pp. 1157, 1158.

4 See note 28 on page 61.

5 'Methods of Bible Study,' in: R Dabrowski, ed., *Statements and Guidelines and Other Documents of the Seventh-day Adventist Church*, published by the General Conference Communication Department, 2005.

6 See vol. 5, pp. 175-181 of the *Seventh-day Adventist Bible Commentary* (1956).

7 The *Adventist Theological Society* (ATS) is associated with the Seventh-day Adventist Church as an independent ministry. According to its website it is 'an international, professional, nonprofit organization established as a theological resource for the Seventh-day Adventist Church.' The association is conservative in its theology and has the confidence of the current top church leadership. This is not (or at least less) true for the Adventist Society of Religious Studies (ASRS), which is considered by many to be quite 'liberal.'

8 See p. 45.

9   Merlin D. Burt, 'History of Seventh-day Adventist Views on the Trinity,' *Journal of the Adventist Theological Society*, 17/1 (Spring 2006), pp. 125–139. See also Richard Rice, 'God,' in: Gary Charter, ed., *The Future of Adventism* (Ann Arbor, MI: Griffin & Lash, Publishers, 2015), pp. 3-24, and Woodrow Whidden, et al., *The Trinity: Understanding God's Love, His Plan of Salvation and Christian Fellowships* (Hagerstown, MI: Review and Herald, 2002).

10 This book resulted from lengthy discussions in 1955-56 between a few representatives of the Adventist Church and two evangelical leaders. Donald Barnhouse and Walter Martin wanted to know more about the teachings of the Seventh-day Adventists, before Martin published a book about Adventism. See George R. Knight, *Seventh-day Adventists Answer Questions on Doctrine—Annotated Edition* (Berrien Springs, MI: Andrews University Press, 2003).

11 For a very accessible summary of Ellen White's many statements about the human nature of Christ, see Dennis Fortin, 'Ellen White and the Human Nature of Christ,' https://www.andrews.edu/~fortind/EGWNatureofChrist.htm

12 See Jean-Claude Verrecchia, *God of No Fixed Address: From Altars to Sanctuaries, Temples to Houses* (Eugene, OR: Wipf and Stock, 2015). This important book explores new paths regarding the sanctuary doctrine. So far it has appeared in English, French and Dutch. Verrecchia pleads for a frank reappraisal of the traditional Adventist view of this doctrine, after stressing the widespread unease among many Adventist believers about the traditional interpretation. For a historical survey of how Adventism has related to the sanctuary doctrine, see Alberto R. Timm, 'The Seventh-day Adventist Doctrine of the Sanctuary (1844-2007), in: Martin Pröbstle et al., eds, *For You Have Strengthened Me: Biblical and Theological Studies in Honor of Gerard Pfandl in Celebration of his Sixty-Fifth Birthday* (Peter am Hart (Austria): Seminar Schloss Bogenhofen, 2007), pp. 331-359.

13 Dr. David Trim, director of the Office of Archives and Statistics of the world-wide Seventh-day Adventist Church, reported to the Annual Council in 2013 the outcome of a research project in which over 4,000 church members around the world participated. 38 percent indicated that they do not (or nor fully) accept the doctrine of the sanctuary and the investigative judgment.

14 A survey of over 200 pastors in 2000 in the Los Angeles (USA) region indicated that 41 percent of them did not accept the traditional version of the Adventist sanctuary doctrine. See Aivars Ozolins, 'Doctrinal Dissonance and Adventist Leadership: Recapturing Spiritual Wholeness through Crisis, http://lasierra.edu/fileadmin/documents/religion/School_of_Religion_2011-12/ASRS_2011/05_Aivars_Ozolins_Doctrinal_Dissonance.pdf.

15 Reinder Bruinsma, *Seventh-day Adventist Attitudes toward Roman Catholicism*, 1844-1965 (Berrien Springs, MI: Andrews University Press, 1994).

PART 2

Facing doubts and finding answers

CHAPTER 6

The leap of faith

Writing the first five chapters was relatively easy. It was a *description* of what I see and experience—in the world around me, and in particular in the religious world of today. It was about the crisis in the Christian church—the Seventh-day Adventist Church most definitely included. Then I moved to the crisis of personal faith that many experience and, in the previous chapter, to the uneasiness many Seventh-day Adventists feel about some of the teachings of their church and about its doctrinal rigidity. At the very beginning of the book I explained that I want to address a specific group of readers: those who feel they are no longer at home in their church and are drifting towards the back door. I called this category the 'believers on the margins.'

But it is one thing to provide a *description* of a situation and quite a different challenge to provide a *prescription* to remedy the spiritual ailment that so many 'on the margins' suffer from—individually and collectively—and to suggest how the church might be restored to full health. In fact, if that is what you expect, you may as well quit reading at this very point, because you will be disappointed. On the previous pages I raised many questions—head-on and between the lines—for which I have no immediate answers. Moreover, although I do not see myself as a 'believer on the margins,' who is slowly drifting towards the exit of organized faith, I do share many of the concerns of the 'marginals' and often feel the same uneasiness about several current trends in Adventism.

What you may expect in this chapter and in the chapters that follow will be an honest attempt to point to some ways of dealing with our (yours and mine) uncertainties and doubts in an open, and, hopefully, constructive way. I have, in past years and in preparation for this book, thought a lot about the issues involved. Over the years I have written a great deal about these topics and talked with many people about them. In what follows I want to present some of my (often tentative) conclusions. I will feel that my efforts have been more than worthwhile if some readers, here and there, find a few pointers helpful in facing their doubts and in dealing constructively with their questions. And I will be delighted if, perhaps, as a result of reading this book some will move away from 'the margins' and find a satisfactory way of participating more fully in the life of the church and of living their faith.

WHAT IS DOUBT?

Let's first of all try to remove a few frequent misconceptions about doubt. Os Guinness, a prominent Christian writer, mentions in the introduction of his book on doubt three of these misconceptions:
1. doubt is wrong, for it is the same as unbelief;
2. doubt is only associated with faith, and not with knowledge; and
3. doubt is something to be ashamed of, and it is dishonest to stay in the church if you have serious doubts.[1]

A little later in his book he makes the important point that doubt is universal: 'Only God and madmen have no doubts,' he says.[2] As we continue we will, hopefully, disarm these misconceptions.

We need to define the concept of doubt a bit further. Doubt is not something that is only found in religion and faith. We may doubt the wisdom of certain professional decisions and choices we have made in the past. We may doubt the conclusions some scholars have arrived at, or doubt the truth of statements made by our political leaders. We may be unsure how to proceed with a particular project or may doubt that we have the necessary expertise. We may have serious doubts about important moral issues. Some people may have doubts about the faithfulness of their spouse. Therefore, if doubt is such a widespread phenomenon, it would be strange if we did not encounter doubt when entering the arena of religion. *Doubt is not just a Christian problem, it is a human problem.*[3]

Doubt is not by definition something negative. It can become destructive and even fatal if we are unwilling to face it, and are reluctant to think about it and struggle with it. It becomes an outright danger for our spiritual health if we cherish our doubts, as if they are conclusive proof of our independent thinking and our superb intelligence, instead of trying to deal with them.

Some of the 'saints' of past and present have gone through periods of great doubt. The story of St Thérèse of Lisieux (1873-1897) is worth reading. A French Carmelite nun, popularly known as 'the Little Flower of Jesus,' she is one of the influential models of sanctity among Roman Catholics, almost on a par with St Francis of Assisi. She died of tuberculosis at the age of 24, after having gone through a period of profound doubt. At a certain moment she confessed she no longer believed in the prospect of eternal life and said that Christ had brought her to an underground space where the sun could no longer penetrate.[4] In spite of her dark period of doubt she was canonized by Pope Pius XI on May 17, 1925, and she is now referred to as a 'doctor of the church.'

Martin Luther experienced a prolonged period of doubt and had an acute sense of the absence of God. He referred to these tribulations as his *Anfechtungen*—a religious crisis that affected his entire being. He admitted later that sometimes, when he wanted to preach, he was so overwhelmed by doubt that the words froze upon his lips.

And to the surprise of many, even Mother Teresa went through long seasons of spiritual dryness and a feeling of being disconnected from God.[5] Although perpetually cheery in public, Teresa went through a period of great spiritual pain. In more than forty letters, many of which have never before been published, she bemoans the 'dryness,' 'darkness,' 'loneliness' and 'torture' she is undergoing. She compares the experience to hell and at one point says it has driven her to doubt the existence of heaven and even of God.[6]

Doubt is not the same as unbelief. It is important to make that distinction. *Unbelief* is a willful, intentional refusal to believe. It is a deliberate refusal to recognize the possibility that God exists and is an explicit rejection of faith. *Doubt* may perhaps best be described as an open-minded uncertainty, while *unbelief* stands for the closed-minded certainty that God and faith are nonsense, or, at the very least, quite irrelevant. I read somewhere (I do not recollect where) that the Chinese speak of someone who doubts as one who has a foot in two boats. The English word *doubt,* as well as the French word *doute,* are derived from the Latin word *dubitare.* It refers to a state of being divided—of being of two minds.

The famous Protestant theologian Paul Tillich (1886-1965) made the oft-quoted statement (which has also been attributed to St Augustine): 'Doubt is not the opposite of faith; it is an element of faith.'[7] The Jewish author Isaac Bashevis Singer (1902-1991) was also quite positive about the value of doubt: 'Doubt is part of all religion. All the religious thinkers were doubters.'[8] Alfred Lord Tennyson (1809-1892), one of Britain's most popular poets in the Victorian era, wrote in his poem *In Memoriam,* 'There lives more faith in honest doubt, believe me, than in half the creeds.'[9]

Tasting a bit of doubt can deepen our faith. It can give us a hardier, more enduring, more resilient faith. Gary Parker said in the book *The Gift of Faith,* 'If faith never encounters doubt, if truth never struggles with error, if good never battles with evil, how can faith know its own power?'[10] Of all the definitions of 'doubt' that I have come across I like the one by Os Guinness perhaps best: *'Doubt is faith being out of focus.'*[11]

IS DOUBT SIN?

Many 'believers on the margins' feel bad, or even outright guilty, about having doubts. Doubting is wrong, they think. Having doubt is a sin. They remember the story of Adam and Eve in paradise and their meeting with the evil one, who approached them in the guise of a snake. The first couple had no reason for doubt—they lived in perfect harmony and total peace in a delightful garden. They had an open line of communication with their Creator. But when the devil enters the scene, doubt comes with him. He suggests that Adam and Eve would be fully justified in doubting God's good intentions. God is holding things back from them, the devil says, which would make them more mature. Can this be true, Adam and Eve wonder. They had not thought of that possibility until that moment and doubt enters their minds—with fateful consequences. Anyone who reads this story will draw a straight line between the devil and sin, on the one hand, and doubt, on the other hand.

In *Steps to Christ,* one of her best known books, Ellen G. White also establishes this direct link between doubt and sin. Chapter 12 of this book is entitled: 'What to do with doubt.' She begins the chapter by admitting that Christians are not immune to doubt.

> *Many, especially those who are young in the Christian life, are at times troubled with the suggestions of skepticism. There are in the Bible many things which they cannot explain, or even understand, and Satan employs these to shake their faith in the Scriptures as a revelation from God. They ask, 'How shall I know the right way? If the Bible is indeed the word of God, how can I be freed from these doubts and perplexities?'*[12]

We note that Satan—the devil—is immediately brought into the picture. It is not hard to find other places where Ellen G. White makes that same connection. Take, for instance, this statement: 'Satan will work ingeniously, in different ways and through different agencies, to unsettle the confidence of God's remnant people.'[13]

Is it correct to link doubt with 'the devil' and with 'sin'? Yes and no. If we assume that everything that is negative and problematic results, in one way or another, from the fact that we are human beings, who have allowed 'evil' to enter our world and to infect our lives, then, yes, that is where doubt has its place. But this would be a very lopsided interpretation. For if we take a good look at other Bible stories, we also get a different picture that shows us the other side of doubt. (We will not, at this point, worry unduly about the *historicity* of the biblical stories, but focus on the *message* they have for us.)

Let us take a look at one of the greatest doubters the Bible mentions, John the Baptist. He was the 'forerunner' of Jesus. When Jesus came to him, while John was baptizing people in the Jordan River, he knew perfectly well who this Jesus was. And he realized that once Jesus started his mission as the Messiah, his own ministry would inevitably collapse. The gospel narratives provide us with only a few details about John and his work, but we meet him again when he is locked up as a prisoner in the Machaerus fortress that King Herod had built near the Dead Sea. John is alive, but has few illusions about his future. He is deeply depressed and his heart is full of doubt. How can it be that he must end his life as a prisoner? He had, like many others around him, believed that this Jesus was the Messiah, who would bring an end to the Roman oppression of his people. However, this had not happened. Jesus had only a small group of followers. He had no permanent place where he could live in reasonable comfort, nor did he have a representative headquarters building where he could receive the leaders of his people and diplomats from surrounding nations, as he was in the process of establishing his reign.

We read in the story that is recorded in Matthew 11:2-14 that John is allowed to send some of his followers to Jesus. At one time he had been so sure: This Jesus was the Lamb of God who was going to take away the sins of the world (John 1:29). But now this certainty has completely evaporated and he sends his disciples to Jesus with the question, 'Are you really the one we expected? Or have we been totally mistaken?' Can there be a more intense doubt than when you have invested your entire life in supporting and promoting someone, because you truly believed in that person, and when at the end you wonder whether it was all a farce, and whether the person you trusted was perhaps an imposter?

Jesus does not scold the men who came to see him on behalf of his cousin John. He simply told them to keep their eyes open, to look around and to report to John what they had seen and heard about his ministry. You would do well to go to this gospel story and read it once again. And, then, do not miss the remark Jesus made about John, in which he put him in the same class as the great Old Testament prophet Elijah: 'Truly, I say to you, among those born of women there has risen no one greater than John the Baptist... From the days of John the Baptist until now the kingdom of heaven has suffered violence, and men of violence take it by force. For all the prophets and the law prophesied until John; and if you are willing to accept it, he is Elijah who is to come' (Matthew 11:11-14). Clearly, Jesus did not see John the Baptist as a hopeless sinner because he was temporarily overcome by serious doubt.

Doubt does not equal sin—at least not sin in the sense of a personal failure that should create guilt in the heart of the doubter. We discover this not only in the story of John the Baptist but also in other stories about biblical doubters. We all know Thomas, one of Jesus' twelve disciples, as the proverbial doubter. We are told that Thomas was not present when the resurrected Christ first appeared to his disciples and that, when Thomas heard reports of Jesus' appearance, he refused to believe that Jesus was indeed alive. Thomas wanted verifiable evidence. Shortly after this, he saw Jesus and touched his wounds. His doubt dissipated and he recognized Jesus for who he was: 'My Lord and my God' (John 20:28).

We have no way of knowing whether the apocryphal story in the *Acts of Thomas*[14] about the death of the apostle Thomas in 72 AD is historical, but some other sources agree that he was killed as a martyr in Mylapore, a district of the Indian city of Chennai. He was taken to a place outside the city, where four soldiers pierced him with their lances. Strong traditions place Thomas in India, where he is said to have preached the gospel from ca. 52 AD onwards. Thomas had an impressive apostolic CV, in spite of the fact that he is portrayed as a doubter in the Gospel of John (20:19-29).

John the Baptist and Thomas are not the only biblical doubters. Think of the stories of Abraham and Sarah, and of Zechariah, the father of John the Baptist. And think of Job. In his misery Job struggled with intense doubt, but he did not abandon God, as his wife suggested. He wondered, Why had this happened to him? It was not fair. How could his misfortunes be reconciled with the picture of a loving and compassionate God? Reading the last few chapters of the book of Job is a very rewarding experience. Job came to the conclusion that, in the final analysis, his doubts were caused by his inadequate concept of God!

(RE-)DISCOVERING FAITH IN GOD

For many the final conclusion of Job is not (yet?) within reach. They continue to struggle with their doubt. If doubt is the halfway point between faith and unbelief (as I believe it is), how can a 'believer on the margins' move towards faith, rather than be drifting ever further away from faith and ending up with sheer unbelief?[15]

It has often been said that having faith in God requires a big *leap*. Paul Ricoeur (1913-2005), the well-known Protestant French philosopher and a renowned expert in the field of hermeneutics (principles of interpretation), urged people to *begin* their spiritual journey with faith, and not with doubts and intellectual efforts to dispel those doubts. He challenged them to start with a 'wager.' We are better off, he said, when we take the calculated risk of assuming that belief in the Christian story will be more fruitful for living in the world than a program of skepticism. It does not mean that we must simply try to forget our doubts and questions, but that we decide to move forward on the basis of a *hypothetical belief.* To do so, we must decide to place ourselves (or ensure that we remain) in an environment where faith is practiced.[16] We must give the Christian story the chance to impress us, and then we should wait and see what it does with us. If we take this 'leap of faith,' we will experience that the proof of the pudding is in the eating.

Our environment has a major influence on our experiences. It is very difficult to enjoy one of the Brandenburg concertos of Johann Sebastian Bach while working in a car repair shop, where all kinds of mechanical and other noises interfere with the beauty of this marvelous example of classical music. If we feel tense and rushed, we will more readily find rest and relaxation during a quiet walk along the beach, or on a pleasant café terrace sipping our cup of cappuccino, than while riding on a full train or trying to beat the rush hour traffic. A candlelit dinner in a cozy restaurant is usually more conducive to romance than standing in line at a McDonald's. The atmosphere of a medieval cathedral, the reading of a spiritual book, a piece of inspiring music, the company of a partner or a good friend who is a genuine believer, being captivated by the beauty of nature—all of these things may create the kind of environment that facilitates a feeling of ultimate dependence on God—the intuitive certainty that there is One who cares.

Ricoeur suggests that faith emerges and grows (and is maintained) best in an environment where the 'language of faith' is spoken. The best way of learning and maintaining proficiency in a language is submerging oneself in that language. This is also true with respect to the language of faith. I agree with Ricoeur on the basis of my own experience. When in 1984 I moved with my family to the West African country of Cameroon, I found that only one person spoke English in the church institution that I had come to direct. The forty or so employees communicated with each other in Bulu—one of the many local languages in this country. The official language was French. I had some basic knowledge of the French language from my secondary school days. However, the first few weeks nearly drove me crazy, as I understood virtually nothing of what the people told me. But I listened and tried to talk with them, even though my grammar was hopelessly defective and my vocabulary extremely minimal. I bought the local newspaper and studied it 'religiously' every evening. I decided to add twenty new words to my French vocabulary every day. After two months or so, the penny quite suddenly dropped. I found that I began to understand what people were saying. After some more time I became reasonably proficient in French and even ventured to preach in this language. However, I must admit that today I have lost much of my French, because I am now only seldom in a French-speaking environment. My experience with the Swedish language is very similar. My wife and I wanted to learn this Scandinavian language for a good reason: our two little granddaughters live in Sweden and speak Swedish rather than Dutch. We have now come to the point where we can talk with them, and as an extra bonus, we can read the superb Wallander crime novels in their original language! Again, the secret was to immerse ourselves in the Swedish language as much as possible.

So, Ricoeur says, if you want to help people who have tried in vain to have faith, advise them to become (and stay) acquainted with the *language of faith*.

If you are among the people who are 'on the margins' and in danger of losing your faith, read the Bible, even though at first it might not mean much to you. Even if you have become weary of the disagreeable things in the Bible, this nonetheless is and remains a good idea. (Just skip, at least for the time being, the sections you find difficult to swallow.) Also: convince yourself to attend church, where you will hear the language of faith, even though many elements in the church service may upset you, and even though you may meet people you would rather stay away from. Listen to the prayers of others and say some prayers yourself, even though you may wonder whether this has any use. Once again: *Immerse yourself in the language of faith.*

Many who have done this have said that they have *received* faith or recovered it. I use the word *receive* on purpose. For, after all, faith is a gift and not something that results from our own hard intellectual labor. We will return later to this aspect.

Many of those who have followed the route that Paul Ricoeur and others have advised will testify that Christianity is true because 'it works.' But, true enough, having faith requires a major *leap!* Some would say that it is a leap in the dark or would even argue that faith is a psychological aberration, a mental dysfunction. Sigmund Freud (1856-1939) was the most famous proponent of that view. He regarded religious belief as mere wishful thinking. And he also used less kind words, such as neurosis, illusion, poison, and intoxicant. God as the heavenly Father is just a projection, he said, derived from our subconscious hang-ups about our human father. Others have said similar things.

Well, Freud and others who thought and think like him are entitled to their opinions. For that is all they are: *opinions*. There is not a scrap of real *evidence* to support their ideas. It should be noted that by putting it all in the realm of the subconscious, Freud's theory is conveniently beyond any kind of verification! Moreover, the suggestion that faith can be reduced to wishful thinking has, upon a little reflection, not much to commend itself. For it is clear that many features of religious belief (e.g. sin and judgment) simply do not correspond to our wildest dreams!

IS THERE A BASIS FOR FAITH IN GOD?

I will try not to become too technical, but our topic demands that we probe a little deeper. In chapter two we saw that few people today are impressed—and convinced—by the classical 'proofs' for the existence of God. As I have personally struggled with the question whether I could be sure that God really exists, I have experienced the truth of the 'method' that Paul Ricoeur recommended. But I have also benefited very much from reading two other important books. During a vacation I saw the first of these two books accidentally (or was it providentially?) in a small bookshop in a provincial town in Sweden. I wondered why it was there amidst just a handful of rather mediocre books on theology and philosophy. I wanted to have something 'serious' to read, and seeing there was not much choice, I bought Nancey Murphy's book, *Beyond Liberalism and Fundamentalism.*[17] I do not remember how I found the second book, *Warranted Christian Beliefs.*[18] It is written by Alvin Plantinga, presently an emeritus professor at the prestigious Catholic Notre Dame University in South Bend, Indiana. These two theologians helped me to relax and to put my questions about God's existence to rest. They told me that there is no hard 'proof' for the existence of God, but that there are nonetheless good arguments for believing he exists. They explain in their books that there is always room for doubt, but that this, in itself, is not an insurmountable problem.

For a Seventh-day Adventist pastor it is, of course, always a good thing to mention that Ellen G. White wholeheartedly agrees with a particular standpoint! And she does indeed in this case. Let me, therefore, before I move on with the more philosophical terminology that I found with Nancey Murphy and Alvin Plantinga, quote a few lines from Steps to Christ, from the chapter I have already quoted from above:

God never asks us to believe, without giving sufficient evidence upon which to base our faith. His existence, his character, the truthfulness of his Word, are all established by testimony that appeals to our reason; and this testimony is abundant. Yet God has never removed the possibility of doubt.[19]

I hope you will continue to have the patience and stamina to stay with me when I leave Ellen G. White and move on to Murphy and Plantinga. They address the question whether there is a firm foundation for our belief in God in depth. Like Ellen G. White they argue that there will always be room for doubt! (If what follows becomes too philosophical for your taste, just feel free to skip the rest of this section.)

How can we be sure that, when we speak about God, we are not merely using pious words, but are actually speaking about a Reality that exists? How can we be certain that we speak about a personal Being, who acts and intervenes in this world in real time? And can we be absolutely sure that the building blocks of the Christian faith are absolutely and undeniably true? Are there at least some moral principles that are timeless and unchangeable?

Foundationalism is the name for the philosophical attempt to discover such absolute principles—beliefs that do not for their justification depend on other beliefs, but are 'basic' or 'immediate.' There are different versions of foundationalism on the market. 'Strong' foundationalists or 'classic' foundationalists build on the conviction that all our knowledge can, indeed, be grounded in some absolute and unassailable principles.[20] According to this theory, those basic beliefs are self-evidently true. In other words: when you meet them they strike you with such force that you cannot but accept them as true. Today, there is widespread doubt about the legitimacy of this 'strong' foundationalism. No one, it is argued, can approach these supposedly 'basic' matters without any preconceptions. And even if several of the principles that seem to be 'basic' support each other, this so-called 'concurrence' does not constitute a watertight proof of their truth.

If this 'strong' foundationalism is a bridge too far, does that mean that there is nothing solid to build on; that there is nothing beyond social customs and personal preferences, and that total skepticism will have to prevail? Fortunately, we can travel the road that is usually referred to as 'modest foundationalism.' According to this approach we must do with less than *absolute* certainty, but there is *enough* certainty on which to ground our faith (once again Ellen G. White would agree, even though she, I am sure, never heard the term *foundationalism*). 'Modest' foundationalists say that their core beliefs are not totally immune to some conceivable doubts, but that they 'are perfectly acceptable, unless one has good reason to think that they have been undermined. They are innocent unless proven guilty.'[21]

Now, please stay with me for a little longer! Many who have studied this topic insist that something may be considered reliable as long as a reliable method has been followed to produce it.[22] If different ideas are consistent with one another and form a coherent whole, there is a good reason to accept them as true. Following this line of thought, there is, however, no assumption that a justified set of beliefs comes in the form of a complete *building,* as such a metaphor would make its truth claim too strong. But beliefs, so Nancey Murphy and other proponents of the 'modest foundationalist' view say, are interdependent—each belief being supported by its connection to other beliefs and ultimately to the whole.[23] The American philosopher W.V. Quine (1908-2000) preferred the metaphor of a *web.*[24] The image of a web suggests that individual threads may be fragile and vulnerable, but that all the threads together can form a solid structure. Thus, individual beliefs may have weaknesses and may be subject to doubt, but a set of coherent beliefs gives us a strong enough basis from which to proceed. Alvin Plantinga (b. 1932) has introduced the notion of '*warranted* beliefs.'[25] He argues that we may not have the absolute certainty for our beliefs that the 'strong' foundationalists are looking for, but that there is sufficient 'warrant' for holding the beliefs that are the basis of Christianity.

Even if an element of wishful thinking were involved, Plantinga argues, that may not actually discredit the notion of faith. Perhaps our Designer-God (assuming that he indeed exists) has constructed us with a kind of inbuilt desire to believe in him and to become more aware of his presence. 'Humans may well be psychologically so constructed by their Maker that, when they undergo certain kinds of experiences, a belief in God is naturally ... the result.'[26] Maybe the great church father Augustine (354-430) was pointing us in that direction with his famous dictum, *Our hearts are restless till they rest in Thee, O God!*[27]

FAITH BEYOND REASON

Before we leave this aspect, let me be clear that everything that parades as faith does not qualify as such. There is a kind of faith that is unwholesome and that depresses people. It makes them feel boxed in and makes them neurotic or fearful. There is the kind of faith that results in the obnoxious arrogance of having the final truth about everything. This kind of faith fosters intolerance and has often led to terrible persecution.

Hans Küng, a Roman Catholic theologian who was, (to put it mildly) not always appreciated by the leaders of his church, stated it very well:

> *Belief in God was and is often authoritarian, tyrannical, and reactionary. It can produce anxiety, immaturity, narrow-minded-ness, intolerance, injustice, frustration and social isolation; it can legitimize and inspire immorality, social abuse and wars within a nation and between nations. But belief in God can also be liberating, oriented on the future and beneficial to human beings; it can spread trust in life, maturity, broadmindedness, tolerance, solidarity, creative and social commitment; spiritual renewal, social reform and world peace.*[28]

This 'liberating' and 'beneficial' kind of faith is the faith we want to have or recover. Only the kind of faith that builds people, that makes them grow as individuals and makes them more human, is worthy of that name.[29]

Some people talk about faith and belief in God as if it is something strange and abnormal, or something that we should by now have outgrown. We must vehemently protest against that notion. We all have faith in lots of things, all the time. When I drive my car across a narrow bridge, I do not hesitate to follow other cars. I do not stop and first launch a meticulous private investigation into the strength of the pillars underneath the structure. The bridge has been there for many years. Hundreds of cars cross it every day. I have strong faith that it will also hold me as I drive across.

We have faith in many other things. I have never been to either the North Pole or the South Pole. (But who knows? I keep on dreaming about a cruise to the Artic regions!) However, I have seen many pictures of people standing with their national flag on the spot they say is the pole. I have no way of checking this. The pictures could have been faked in Northern Canada or Siberia, or been photo-shopped by a computer whiz kid in Miami. But I am not a member of the 'flat-earth society' and believe that the world is a globe and that there are two points at opposite sides that we call the 'poles.' I do not doubt that quite a few people have managed to get there by various means. Likewise, when we take the bus or get on a plane, we have faith in the skills of the driver or the pilot, and when we go to a restaurant we have faith that the chef will not poison us.

H.C. Rümke (1893-1967), one of the most prominent Dutch psychiatrists of the mid-twentieth century, made a strong case for the normality of religious belief in his classic book about character and disposition in relationship to belief and unbelief.[30] If we define faith as trusting something to be true, and as acting on that trust, without definitive intellectual evidence, we must conclude, he says, that there are no people who do not have faith. Our entire existence is based on that kind of trusting faith that is not unlike instinct or intuition. Religious belief is a particular form of faith. To suggest that this kind of faith is evidence of mental dysfunction or of a lack of maturity shows an unreasonable bias.[31]

Faith, it appears, cannot be equated with the intellectual acceptance of logical arguments or certain indubitable propositions. And not even Plantinga's reasoning of 'warranted beliefs' will take away all clouds of doubt. The belief that God exists and that we can have faith in him (i.e. that we can trust him) goes beyond what we can argue with our minds, however brilliant we may think we are, and it goes beyond what we can see, hear or feel. This is what the author of the Letter to the Hebrews underlines in his famous definition of faith: 'Faith is the assurance of things hoped for, the conviction of things not seen' (Hebrews 11:1). Or, as Eugene Peterson paraphrases it in his *Message Bible*, 'Faith is the firm foundation under everything that makes life worth living for. It's our handle on what we can't see.'[32] This definition does not imply that we have to say 'good bye' to reason and intelligence. It does not mean that Mark Twain was right when he said, 'Faith is believing what you know ain't true!' Faith is not a matter of leaving our intellect behind and a willingness to enter a world of magic or science fiction in which everything is possible.

Skeptics who want to doubt everything, will, of course, continue to argue that faith must be based on solid evidence, i.e. on proof that can be checked by the use of our senses. But there is always a fatal inconsistency in the actions and reasoning of the skeptic: in concrete situations the skeptic, who believes he cannot be sure of anything, invariably leaves his skepticism behind. When his house is on fire he will not doubt the reality of the fire but will call the emergency number, grab a few valuables and get out of the house!

Naturally, reason is important, but, when push comes to shove, why should we just trust one of the many faculties with which we have been endowed, and not also other faculties we are equipped with? Why should we, for instance, trust reason more than perception or intuition? The choice to rely purely on reason is, when everything is said and done, an arbitrary decision.[33] Faith, Hans Küng says, 'would be half a thing were it only to address our understanding and reason and not the whole person, including our hearts.' It is not primarily a matter of theological statements or doctrines as defined by a church, or of intellectual arguments, but has also much to do with our imagination and emotions.[34]

Belief in God is not without challenges, but it is worth 'trying to believe.'[35] 'We may feel we have too little evidence to be certain. But, on the other hand, we also have too much evidence to ignore.'[36] We may not have final proof, but so far no one has produced a convincing proof for the non-existence of God either. Believing in God is an act of the human person as a whole, of reason and heart; an act of reasonable trust for which there may not be strict proofs, but for which there are good reasons!

A GOD WE CAN BELIEVE IN?

We must now take another step—or *leap*—in our quest for faith. An important question we must address is whether our faith is directed towards the *true* God. Christian faith has first of all to do with trust in a *person.* Some mistakenly center their faith on the Bible and make the Scriptures into their god. Many Christians have made that error. Many Protestants worship a book rather than a Person; they place their faith in a document rather than in the One to whom the document refers. Many Roman Catholics commit the mistake of making their church the focus of their faith, rather than the One whom the church has been called to proclaim.[37] Some Adventists have centered their faith on the twenty-eight *Fundamental Beliefs.* We must never forget, however, that *genuine faith is a person-to-Person relationship.* Everything else is secondary.

But then, of course, the pivotal question returns: *Can we believe in a God who allows so many terrible things to happen?* There is no easy answer to this question. In fact, there is no conclusive answer at all. Ultimately, the only human response can be, If God is love and knows everything, he knows what he is doing. He must have his reasons for letting evil run its course in the world. Yes, he is almighty. He *can* do all things, but he *chooses* the things he does. He chooses to enlist his power in his own inscrutable ways. If God is the kind of God the Bible claims he is, he is all-wise, and his wisdom is to be trusted—however challenging that trust may be when disaster strikes.

I know of no biblical story that illustrates this point better than that of Job, the patriarch who, at the beginning of the story, had all he wanted and then lost everything: his material possessions, his home, his health, and even his children. No wonder he asked the eternal question, *Why?* His 'friends' pretended to know the answer. They argued that there had to be some terrible secret in Job's life, for which he was being punished by God. Job himself was at a loss to understand why he had fallen on such hard times. His wife advised him to quit believing in God.

Admittedly, there are some very remarkable aspects in this tale of loss and recovery. First of all, there is something I find very hard to understand in this book of the Bible. In the first chapter Satan is introduced as an important player. Strangely enough, the devil still has access to heaven and we read that he can still appear in the presence of God. He argues with God about Job and Job's egoistic reasons for being loyal to God. As a result of this discussion God allows Satan to test Job—even though God sets a limit: Satan cannot take Job's life. I must admit that I find it an odd story, but the essential meaning must be that there is much more involved in the mystery of evil, suffering and death than we can see and understand. This Old Testament story tells us that there is a super-human dimension to the problem of evil and suffering, and that, therefore, we must not presume that we, as limited human beings, can find conclusive answers.

But then there is the final section of the book of Job. It is one of my favorite parts of the Bible. It tells us that God can never be defined, since he is infinitely different from us, and infinitely greater than we will ever be able to imagine. When Job's friends have no more words and Job himself sees no way out of his dilemma, God speaks to him 'from a violent storm' and makes his point by asking Job a long series of intriguing questions:

> Why do you confuse the issue?
> Why do you talk without knowing what you're talking about?
> Pull yourself together, Job! Up on your feet! Stand tall!
> I have some questions for you,
> and I want some straight answers.
>
> Where were you when I created the earth?
> Tell me, since you know so much!

Who decided on its size?
Certainly you'll know that!
Who came up with the blueprints and measurements?
How was its foundation poured, and who set the cornerstone? ...
And have you ever ordered Morning, 'Get up!' told Dawn, 'Get to work!' ...
so you could seize Earth like a blanket
and shake out the wicked like cockroaches? ...

Have you ever gotten to the true bottom of things,
explored the labyrinthine caves of the deep ocean?
Do you know the first thing about death?
Do you have one clue regarding death's dark mysteries?
And do you have any idea how large this earth is?
Speak up if you have even the beginning of an answer.

(Job 38, The *Message* paraphrase)

I have only quoted a few of the long list of questions God addressed to Job. Job clearly gets the message. His complaints cease. He is at long last able to see things in the right proportions:

Job answered God: 'I'm convinced: You can do anything and everything. Nothing and no one can upset your plans... I babbled on about things far beyond me, made small talk about wonders way over my head. You told me, "Listen, and let me do the talking. Let me ask the questions. You give the answers." *I admit I once lived by rumors of you; now I have it all firsthand - from my own eyes and ears!* I'm sorry - forgive me. I'll never do that again, I promise! I'll never again live on crusts of hearsay, crumbs of rumor.'

(Job 42:1-6, The *Message* paraphrase; italics are mine.)

I will not get into an argument about whether or not the story of Job is historical in all its details. To me it is rather unimportant whether or not in patriarchal times there was an actual man called Job, who owned exactly seven thousand sheep and goats and three thousand camels, and who had a wife, seven sons and three daughters. I do not worry unduly whether the entire story about what happened to him is historically accurate. In any case, it is hard to believe that Job's 'friends' talked to him in the way their speeches are presented in the book of Job. A discussion about the historicity may be interesting but misses the point as to why this 'book' was included in the biblical canon. It became part of the biblical canon because of its perspective on human suffering. It tells us that suffering is real and can leave us broken and in despair. It also underlines the fact that all human theories remain empty and unsatisfactory—as we must conclude when we hear the bombastic words of Job's friends. However, it also wants to convince us that God has the last word. God is presented as the One who can be trusted because of who he is.

I repeat: Christian faith has first of all to do with trust in a 'person.' We will have to admit that we cannot—and never will in this life— understand why God does not interfere when 'bad things happen to good people.' At the same time we should recognize that he does, in fact, interfere much more often than we recognize. If evil is utterly destructive, we owe it to God's constant loving interventions that we are still alive and, in spite of all misery, can experience a lot of joy and beauty. *The mystery of why there is still so much good is perhaps as great as the mystery of why there is so much evil.* As we think about these things, let us always remember that God must be and must always remain God. If we could fully understand him, he would no longer be God, but would be brought down to our level. And who needs that kind of God?

At this point we need to take yet another leap of faith! If God—as Christians see him and the Bible describes him—exists, and if the words of John 3:16 are true, 'that God gave his only son,' we are faced with a sacrifice so immense, and so far beyond any human comprehension, that we must ask ourselves whether we are justified in having doubts about God because of the bad things that happen to us personally and that happen in the world. If it is true that God gave up what was dearest to him on our behalf, we should pause and think twice before we accuse him of not showing enough love towards us. If we can believe that God sacrificed the One who was dearest to him, for our sake, we have indeed a solid basis on which to place our trust in God.

HOW TO GET FAITH IF YOU WANT IT?

We must for a moment go back to the question where and how faith originates. Can you simply choose to have faith? Or choose not to have it? Are some people born with a special capacity to have faith? Is it mainly a matter of environment and upbringing? Why is it that some people would like to get away from their faith and do not succeed in casting it off, while others say they envy people who have faith, but claim they do not know how to obtain such faith for themselves? Those are far from simple questions.

But would it be unreasonable to believe that, if he truly exists and is somehow responsible for our origin, God designed us with a capacity for faith? In other words, that there is something in us that recognizes the fact that God is there and reaches out to us—that he wants to commune with us. Call it a sixth or seventh sense, or give it a Latin name, like the sixteenth century church reformer John Calvin did[38]—or describe it as an inner certainty that there is a God who not only exists, but who cares—whatever you call it, it is there. Could we perhaps say that when people fail to stay attuned to this sense of a divine presence, their antenna becomes so rusty that the signal no longer comes through?

The capacity to receive and give love seems rather similar, I think, to the capacity for religious belief. For most people love is something natural. From the first moments of their lives, even before they can walk and talk, children are able to respond to the love-signals of their mother. We are at a loss to explain this astounding love-mechanism. But it is there. Unless there is some personality disorder, or unless something goes terribly wrong in our childhood years, we grow up with this mysterious capacity to recognize love, to receive and to give it. Love, we might say, is a *gift* we have been given. It does not depend on intellectual arguments, even though we know we should not love without using our brain. Yet, there are degrees in the capacity of people to give and receive love. Some people no longer seem to have the antenna for receiving signals of love from others and somehow are unable to respond to such signals. But this does not lead us to doubt the reality and normality of love.

Faith—the capacity to believe and utterly trust in God and the intense desire to know more about him and to learn what he wants for us and from us—is also a *gift*. Everyone has received this gift to a greater or lesser degree. Paul, a biblical author who wrote a series of letters to some of the mid-first century Christian churches, suggests that God has from the very beginning implanted some basic knowledge about himself in the minds of all people. He points specifically to nature as a source of awareness of God, when he states, 'For ever since the world was created, people have seen the earth and sky. Through everything God made, they can clearly see his invisible qualities—his eternal power and divine nature. So they have no excuse for not knowing God' (Romans 1:20 NLT).

This awareness of the divine does not come as the result of deep thinking or from reading sophisticated philosophical books, or even through a diligent study of the Bible, though all these things have their place. It comes to us as a *gift*. And if we have lost it, it may be retrieved. The apostle Paul, whom we just quoted, also wrote to another local church about the concepts of grace and faith as gifts from God (Ephesians 2:8). This gift may, somehow, just drop as it were from the skies, but as a rule we do well to go to those places where the gift is most commonly 'handed out.'

People who have started to believe will tell you different stories about how they became believers. Some will say that deep down they have always been believers, but for some time they have not been aware of it. Others will be able to pinpoint a precise moment at which they first experienced faith. Still others cannot tell you exactly how they came to believe. But people who talk to you about the history of their faith usually do not refer to intellectual arguments, although these often have provided further depth to their faith. When pointing to when and where their faith started they almost always talk in a language of sense perception. They say they *felt* a divine presence; or they were overwhelmed by *looking* at the starry sky during a clear night. They speak in terms of *awe,* of being *touched* in their innermost self. They suddenly felt they should pray and felt that their prayers were *heard.* Et cetera. There is no doubt that faith has a strong experiential component. It reaches into our mind, but certainly also into our affections.

Can we *decide* that we will have faith, or that we want to go back to the faith we once had, and can we also *refuse* to have faith in God? Let me quote Rümke again:

> I have never been able to observe a case in which someone found faith through thinking or willing. When we look at those who say that they have been brought to faith by rational argument, we always find that the term 'rational' has to be taken in a very loose sense. In further discussions they will often agree that the thought process contained several links which are identical with believing trust.

> In studying those who say that they have acquired faith through their will, I have often discovered that their faith was not genuine, or that this will to believe was, in actual fact, already a form of faith that had somehow developed.

> I cannot say that it is absolutely impossible that there are cases where reason and will have led to faith. I can only say that I have never encountered such cases. But I do think that 'thinking' and 'willing' can play an important role in the inner processing of our experience and in the place we attribute to religion.[39]

The metaphor of a *leap of faith* is very fitting. Faith has often been described as an adventure, or as starting on a path without knowing where it will take you. That was the kind of faith that, according to the story in the Bible, Abraham had, after he was 'called' by God to leave the town where he had settled and to travel to an unknown destination. He did not have the precise coordinates to put in his GPS, so that he could simply follow the Hebrew-speaking male or female voice, programmed to give him instructions at every crossroads or roundabout. He received his roadmap in small segments. Abraham's story illustrates that faith contains an element of adventure. Yet this faith adventure is not a blind leap in the dark, over an abyss of totally unknown width. The sort of things we are asked to believe are not at all like the strange phenomena in the world of Haruki Marukami or Harry Potter. They may not be open to sense verification or laboratory inspection, but they are part of a web of 'justified beliefs' and fit together in a coherent story.

How do you take this leap? Or, to use the other metaphor again, where do you go to receive the 'gift' of faith? I cannot propose a twelve-step program that will help you move from unbelief to belief. It does not work that way. But I believe it is a 'warranted' assumption that God designed us with a capacity for faith, and that he is more than prepared to give the gift of faith once more to those who have somehow lost it. But might he sometimes wait until he feels the occasion is right? Does God perhaps wait until the human receiver has the appropriate attitude, an openness and appreciation for the gift? Above anything else we must remember that faith requires expectation and openness. We must hold out our hand, if we want to have the gift. We must be willing to step forward, and take the leap.

And we must pray. If we have stopped praying, we must get back into the habit of prayer. Of course, I can hear the immediate objection, 'Prayer does not precede faith but follows faith. Believers pray. Unbelievers do not pray.' In a sense that is correct. Those who have faith in God want to talk to the One in whom they believe. But, at the same time, it is also true that prayer may lead to faith. If there is this God who wants us to have faith, would he not have an open ear for even the most primitive of prayers that says, 'Dear God, please, give me that gift'? And if we feel our faith is weak and know not, or no longer, how to pray, should we not repeat the short prayer of the desperate man who came to Jesus when his son was about to die: 'I do believe; help me overcome my unbelief'? (Mark 9:24).

GOD CAN BE FOUND

The good news for 'believers on the margins,' who have trouble believing in God, and in trusting him when they see so much madness and suffering in the world, is that doubt can be overcome and that our doubt can in fact help us to grow into mature, healthy, and balanced believers. I recommend that, if you want examples of people who have conquered their doubts about God, and who found God (either for the first time or after they went through a God-less period), you look for books that tell the stories of people who have found God. These books abound. I have been very encouraged by reading John M. Mulder's book *Finding God.*[40] And thinking about the suffering in the world that causes so much doubt, I have found C.S. Lewis book *The Problem of Pain* very inspiring. Lewis, who was not spared when it comes to suffering, makes this striking remark that gives ample food for thought: 'I have seen great beauty of spirit in some who were great sufferers. I have seen men grow better not worse by advancing years, and I have seen the last illness produce treasures of fortitude and meekness from most unpromising subjects.'[41]

Unfortunately, many people lose their faith, and they do so for different reasons. But the reverse is also true. Many men and women (re-)discover faith and are able to make it a central part of their life. If you are a 'believer on the margins,' I urge you: Do not abandon your faith. God exists and you can have a personal relationship with him that gives new meaning to your life. If your faith has gradually been eroded or has even disappeared, start looking again for the 'gift' of faith. In spite of all my own doubts and uncertainties I still believe this is the best thing a person can do.

---

1   Os Guinness, *Doubt: Faith in Two Minds* (Tring, UK: Lyon Publishing, 1976), p. 15.
2   Ibid. p. 31.
3   Bobby Conyway, op. cit., p. 46.
4   The Czech priest-author Tomás Halík refers at length to Thérèse of Lisieux in his beautiful book *Patience with God: The Story of Zacchaeus Continuing in Us* (New York–London-Toronto-Sydney-Auckland: Doubleday, 2009). See, in particular, chapter 3.
5   See: Brian Kolodiechuk, ed., *Mother Teresa: Come Be My Light: The Private Writings of the Saint of Calcutta* (New York: Doubleday, 2007).
6   http://time.com/4126238/mother-teresas-crisis-of-faith/.
7   Paul Tillich, *Systematic Theology,* 1975, vol. 2, p. 116.
8   *New York Times,* 3 December, 1978.

9   The full text of this long poem is found online in many places. See e.g.: http://www.online-literature.com/tennyson/718/

10 Gary Parker, *The Gift of Doubt: From Crisis to Authentic Faith* (New York: HarperCollins, 1990), p. 69.

11 Guinness, op. cit., pp. 61ff.

12 Ellen G. White, *Steps to Christ*, p. 105.

13 Ellen G. White, *Selected Messages*, p. 48

14 The text of the apocryphal 'Acts of Thomas,' may be found at: http://www.earlychristianwritings.com/text/actsthomas.html.

15 In much of what follows in this chapter I rely on two of my earlier publications: *Faith: Step by Step* (especially chapter 3, pp. 51-66), which was published in 2006 by Stanborough Press, Grantham, UK) and *Keywords of the Christian Faith* (Hagerstown, MD: Review and Herald, 2008), especially chapter 2, pp. 22-31.

16 Robert C. Greer, *Mapping Postmodernism: A Survey of Christian Options* (Downers Grove, IL: InterVarsity Press, 2003), pp. 183, 184

17 Published by Trinity Press in Harrisburg, PA in 1996.

18 Published by Oxford University Press, Oxford/New York, in 2000.

19 *Steps to Christ*, p.102.

20 W. Jay Wood, *Epistemology: Becoming Intellectually Virtuous* (Downers Grove, IL: IVP Academic, 1998), p. 83.

21 Ibid., p. 99.

22 Jonathan Dancy, *Introduction to Contemporary Epistemology* (Oxford, UK: Blackwell, 1985), pp. 31-32.

23 Nancey Murphy, *Beyond Liberalism and Fundamentalism: How Modern and Postmodern Philosophy Set the Theological Agenda* (Harrisberg, PA: Trinity Press International, 1996), p. 94.

24 W.V. Quine and J.S. Ulian, *The Web of Belief* (New York: McGraw-Hill Inc., 1976 ed.).

25 *Warranted Christian Belief* (New York/Oxford: Oxford University Press, 2000).

26 See Alvin Plantinga, op. cit., pp. 192-198; W. Jay Wood, ibid., p. 162.

27 Augustine, *Confessions* (London, UK: Penguin Classics, 1961 ed.), p. 21.

28 Hans Küng, *Credo* (London: SMC Press, transl. R.S. Pine-Coffin, 1993 ed.), p. 14.

29 Anny Matti, *Moeite met God* (Kampen, the Netherlands: J.H. Kok Uitgevers-maatschappij,1991), p. 48.

30 H. C. Rümke, *Karakter en Aanleg in Verband met het Ongeloof* (Kampen: Kok Agora, 2003 ed.).

31 Ibid., pp. 29-34.

32 Eugene H. Peterson. *The Message: The New Testament in Contemporary Language* (Colorado Springs, CO: Navpress, 1993), p. 471.

33 Plantinga, op. cit., 217-222.

34 Küng, op. cit., pp. 7-11.

35 Cf. the title of Nathan Brown's book. See p. 17.

36 Nathan Brown, op. cit., p. 13.

37 Küng, op. cit., p. 11.

38 John Calvin, one of the key leaders of sixteenth century Protestantism, used the term *sensus divinatis*, i.e. an inner awareness of the divine presence.

39 Rümke, op. cit., pp. 37f.

40 Published by William B. Eerdmans in Grand Rapids, MI, 2012.

41 C.S. Lewis, *The Problem of Pain* (Glasgow, UK: Collins, 1989 ed.), p. 86.

CHAPTER 7

Why we must remain in the church

It was in 1985, a few months after my arrival as a 'missionary' of the Seventh-day Adventist Church in Yaoundé, the capital of the West African country of Cameroon. I guess I was not immune to culture shock: living and working in a totally different culture with different habits and rules, coping with a new kind of job, having to endure a hot and humid climate and being forced to communicate in the French language was very challenging. But my greatest problem probably was that I had come with a rather naïve and romantic view of the church in this part of the world. I was accustomed to the materialism of Western Europe. I thought I had left this behind, when our plane lifted from the runway in Amsterdam, but nothing could have been further from the truth. In Africa nothing, absolutely nothing—and that also applies to the church—happens unless money is exchanged.

It did not take me long to find out that in many cases not paying a bribe (giving a *petit cadeau*—a small 'present') was hardly a viable option if I wanted to have something done. It took me not much longer to discover that corruption was also rampant in the Adventist Church. One of the officials in the national headquarters office was involved in an extended, but rather shady, second-hand car import business. Another leader of the church had defrauded the church by a significant amount—significant even by Western standards. He was not sacked, but was re-assigned to the denominational college to serve as a teacher of ethics. (No, I am not making this up!)

So, it was perhaps not so strange that at a given moment I felt somewhat depressed. One afternoon I had some business in town and decided to stop for a coffee at one of the cafés along the Boulevard Kennedy—the main shopping street of Yaoundé. Shortly after I had sat down with my *grand café noir*, I was greeted by a missionary of another denomination, whom I had already met a few times. I invited him to join me at my table for a chat. When he asked me how things were going for me, I took the opportunity to share with him some of my concerns and I told him how disappointed I was in the many deplorable things I was beginning to notice in my church. His response was rather surprising. 'Oh,' he said, 'I have been in this country now for quite a few years and I do actually know quite a bit about what happens in your church. But if you think the situation in the Adventist Church is bad, let me tell you, in my church it is a lot worse. The president of my church runs a brothel!' This openhearted comment greatly encouraged me! After all, my church might have its deficiencies, but it was not the worst!

Well, I could tell you numerous other horror stories. You cannot work for the church for over forty years, and sit countless hours on administrative boards, without regularly hearing about situations that make you want to throw up. And I cannot claim to be perfect myself. I have always tried to be honest and decent, but I must admit that I regret some of the unwise decisions I made in the institutions where I was in charge—decisions that have sometimes hurt people or damaged the church's reputation. I could add that at times I have myself also been hurt by the way in which church members have treated me and by some painful accusations. I have been called names and some have even suggested that I am a Jesuit intruder in the Adventist Church. (If you doubt this, check the Internet. But, even if I wanted to be one, I would not know how to get recruited!)

I realize that many 'believers on the margins' could tell far worse tales about how they have been treated by a church organization or by church members—stories that often make me cringe. Many have suffered grave injustices, have been the victims of vicious slander, shameful discrimination or intolerance, or have been treated with disrespect and indifference. In chapter two we saw how the Christian church has often failed to meet the expectations of the people and we discussed some of the main reasons why people have left organized religion *en masse*. In chapter three we concluded that the Adventist Church is in crisis for many of the same reasons as Christianity in general. However, in spite of all that—and in spite of some rather sad personal experiences, *I want to stay with my church*. And in this chapter I want to challenge all 'believers on the margins' to stay with me in the Adventist Church or to return to it. I believe it is well worth doing so—even though it may not always be easy.

DO WE NEED THE CHURCH?

Often we hear people say, 'I believe in God, but I don't need the church for that. Faith is a personal relationship between God and me, and I do not need the church to stay in touch with God.' This may be true—at least to a certain degree. I know of people who have been steadfast in their faith, even when they were totally isolated from others. I think of Meropi Gijka. She died in 2001 at the ripe age of 97. I had the privilege of meeting her during one of my many visits to Albania in the period when I worked in the regional office of the Seventh-day Adventists Church that, at the time, served thirty-eight countries. Albania was one of these countries. I actually facilitated Meropi's visit to the General Conference session in 1995 in Utrecht.

Meropi had learned about Adventism from an American missionary who worked for a short time in Albania (and who was imprisoned and died there for his faith), shortly before Albania was cut off from the rest of the world, to be ruled by Enver Hoxha, the cruel Communist dictator, who banished all forms of religion from his country. Even possessing a Bible could put a person in mortal danger. For almost fifty years Meropi remained a faithful believer, secretly reading her Bible, which she had carefully hidden. She had one great wish: that the time would come when she could be baptized and that there would be a church in Albania, where she would be able to worship together with other Adventist believers. While she was waiting for that to happen, she faithfully put her tithes in a tin box, which she hid under her bed and which she handed to the first representatives of the Adventist Church who visited the country after the fall of Enver Hoxha. For me Meropi is the undeniable proof of the fact that one does not need the church to be a believer. However, it is nonetheless my firm opinion that, under normal circumstances, faith in God and belonging to a community of believers go together. There is ample proof that not being part of a faith community frequently leads to a gradual weakening, or even disappearance, of one's faith.

If you believe in God and want to have a cordial relationship with him, I think there are at least seven reasons why you should consider it an important privilege to be a member of a faith community.

1. We have been created as social beings, 'made' to be together and to do things together.

There is a strong tendency in today's world to do things alone. Have you noticed how many young people nowadays choose to stay single and to live alone? Of the seventeen million inhabitants in the Netherland 2.7 million live by themselves. But even if we share a home with some other people, we do many things alone. Just think of the amounts of time young (but also not so young) people spend in front of their computer screen or in fiddling with their smartphone. Yes, we live in a time of individualism.

On the other hand, most people also like to be together with other people. They go to big events; they enjoy music festivals or soccer matches, where they can be together with thousands of others. And they want to be in touch with others through the social media. Having a few hundred Facebook 'friends' is quite common, and having more than a thousand is not exceptional.

Christians must strive for balance. They need time alone to nurture their faith. But it is only natural to look for others who also believe that faith is an important facet of their lives. The church is the facilitator of this being-together with other believers.

2. We need the support of others

That is a simple fact of life. We need the support of others, especially when we face major problems or challenges. Have you ever tried to lose weight, all by yourself? Why would millions around the world join *Weight Watchers* or some similar group or organization? Why are there so many support groups for people who have a physical handicap? And why are there so many patient associations, for sufferers of diabetes, cancer, COPD, et cetera? People find support in joining others who are in similar circumstances, especially when they go through crisis situations. It is because we all need encouragement and support, and because together we have a better chance of success in pulling through a difficult situation.

In the past the Adventist Church organized 'five-day-plans' to help people break their smoking addiction. The church started these innovative activities at a time when few organizations bothered about the dangers of tobacco. Why were these activities so successful? It was because the individual efforts of the participants were supported by a group. The people who desperately wanted to stop smoking were in it together.

A number of years ago I participated in a walking event in the Netherlands. Each year some 40,000 people take part in this four-day adventure and walk 30, 40 or 50 kilometers a day, depending on their age. I was in the 40-kilometer bracket. To the surprise of many, I completed the 160 kilometers successfully, without even any blisters. I am, however, sure, I would not have made it had I been on my own. I would probably have given up on day three—the 'day of the seven hills'—if not before. But I could keep going, because I was together with three colleagues. Together we all reached the finish.

I believe that, as a rule, we also need other people to keep going spiritually. And other people must be able to count on us for spiritual support. As one author put it; 'Religion is a team sport.'[1]

3. We complement each other
All parts of our physical body have a very specific role. When I was around forty, I was at times accused of being somewhat of a workaholic, and I cannot deny there was some truth to that. If I was concerned about any aspect of my health, it was mostly about my

heart. People told me, 'Be careful, slow down; one of these days you will have a heart attack.' Over the years I have discovered that I also have other organs, such as a gall bladder and a prostate gland, which can give serious problems. We cease to function properly if any of our vital organs no longer work in the way they should.

It is the same in the 'body of Christ.' The Bible uses a whole range of different metaphors to describe the nature and functioning of the church. The one that refers to the church as a 'body' appeals most to me. Every one of us, whether or not we are 'on the margins' of the church, has certain gifts and talents, while it is equally true that we all lack other important skills and abilities. It means that I can never say that the church can function just as well without me. The truth is that it cannot! We are all needed because we complement each other. In itself this may not be enough of a reason to keep us in the church, or to make us go back, but it does merit serious consideration.

4. Doing things together gives joy and satisfaction
Most people enjoy celebrating special occasions with others—with relatives, friends or colleagues. Weddings, job anniversaries, reunions, birthday parties, are important to them. I always enjoy watching (on television) the 'last night of the Proms' in the Royal Albert Hall in London. It definitely does something to me to see the enthusiasm and the energy that is released, when the entire audience joins in singing *Land of hope and glory – mother of the free.*

You can sing when you are home alone in your bathroom, and pray as you drive to work, and talk on the phone to a friend. But to sing together, to pray together, to discuss things together, to enjoy each other's company, and to comfort each other when there is sadness—it all gives an extra dimension to our life as Christians. The church is the place where all of that takes place.

5. Some blessings can only be experienced in church
Some Christian activities do not require the company of others. You can read your Bible any day of the week, whenever you can spare a few moments. If you are into meditation, you need times and places

of quiet solitude. But other things can only happen when you are together with others. Baptism is a prime example. It is the public acknowledgment of our commitment to Jesus Christ and of our faith in him. It seals our decision to put our trust in God and to try to live in accordance with Christian values. That is true enough, but in the New Testament baptism is also linked with becoming part of a faith community. The apostle Paul said that we are 'baptized into one body' (1 Corinthians 12:13). It is an experience that has a deep meaning for our personal life. But at the same time it connects us with fellow-believers in the church.

One of the central worship activities in the Christian church is the communion service, also often referred to as the Lord's Supper. Roman Catholics and some other denominations speak of the Eucharist or the mass. 'Theologies of communion' differ greatly. Some see the Lord's Supper as a kind of repetition or re-enactment of the sacrifice of Christ, while for others it is strictly symbolic. Most Protestants, however—Adventists included—do not believe that sacraments, as for instance the Lord's Supper, have any magical powers. But the majority of people who participate in the communion service will say that it is very meaningful. They may not be able to describe exactly what it is that makes the eating of a small morsel of bread and the sipping of a little wine so special, but they somehow sense that it strengthens and encourages them, and that it is essential for their pilgrimage of faith.

Of course, it is possible to meditate on the sacrifice of Christ while you have a private walk along the beach. You can stay at home and read the gospel account of the last week of Jesus' life, or listen to Bach's *St Matthew's Passion*. But sitting at the Lord's table is one of the greatest blessings that comes with belonging to the church.

6. We need the church to grow spiritually
If we want to grow and be physically healthy we must eat the right kind of food. This is also true in a spiritual respect. Moving away from 'the margins' of the church requires some initiatives that gather momentum when they are undertaken collectively. We can be revived, grow spiritually and deal with our doubts when we hear God's Word

being preached, read the Bible together and participate in liturgical moments.

It is frequently said that the sermon is a totally outmoded vehicle of communication. Why should a large number of people silently listen to what one man (or woman) has to say? Even if the speaker is well prepared, and is eloquent in an above average measure, the sermon does not score high on the scale of appreciation of a lot of churchgoers. Nevertheless, I believe that somehow the sermon is more than a 30-minute monologue or a lecture about a religious subject. When the Word of God is preached in the context of a worship service, what is said receives added value. Through the centuries churchgoers have felt that through the words of the preacher, the Word of God may come to them. Listening to a sermon is part of exposing ourselves to the language of faith (as we discussed in the previous chapter) and this can become very meaningful if approached with an open heart and mind.

7. Finally, Christians have been given the mandate to proclaim the gospel to the world.
If it is true that God exists, and if we believe that he has shown his infinite care for us by giving his Son, Jesus Christ, for us, it is essential to communicate this 'good news' to others. In biblical terms this kind of communication is referred to as 'witnessing.' It is something that is, first of all, done on a one-to-one basis. Christian believers must have the conviction and the courage to share their faith with the people around them. But the 'gospel commission' involves more than this. It also demands a group-enterprise, with organization, strategies, physical facilities, and financial and personnel resources. This is one of the main reasons for the existence of the church: to share the knowledge of God, and to tell the world, as effectively as possible, about the things God does for us. No one who himself believes in the gospel news can ignore this crucial aspect of being a believer!

WHERE IS THE CHURCH THAT I WOULD WANT TO BE PART OF?
As you are reading this, you may say, This is all going a bit too quick for me. What was said in the previous section might echo with me, if

I just knew a church where I could experience all the good things you just mentioned. The reality is that many 'believers on the margins,' even if they have kept their faith in God or have found it again, have serious problems with organized religion and do not, or no longer, think highly of their church. This has led to an exodus from the church and has created challenges of crisis proportions in most Christian denominations, the Adventist Church not excepted. There may be many among the 'believers on the margins' who would be eager to be part of a community where they can truly have a sense of belonging and where they can have the inner certainty of being at home. If only they could find a place that they can truly experience as their spiritual home.

Many have become utterly frustrated by what they have experienced in their local church and by what they see and hear in their denomination. They have had enough of the narrow-mindedness they have encountered. They have not felt that the life and activities in their church were helpful for them to grow spiritually. Much of what is going on in the church seems shallow or irrelevant to them. They have not felt the joy and satisfaction of being church members and have not experienced the spiritual support that was referred to in such glowing terms in the previous paragraph. In view of this, is it really worth spending time and energy to (re-)connect with the church—the Adventist Church in particular? Does it offer enough to make this worthwhile?

Part of the answer to these questions is based on a correct idea of what the church actually is. We use the word 'church' in several ways. It can stand for religion in general, for instance when we speak about the relationship between 'church' and 'state.' It often refers to a building: a majestic cathedral or a small country church and everything in between. The word church is also used for 'denomination.' Catholics, Lutherans, Baptists and Adventists all speak of 'my church.' It may have the connotation of church organization. This is how I use the word when I say that I hope that 'the church' will continue to send me my monthly retirement check. The term 'invisible church' may refer to all Christians, of all ages. In the biblical writings, however, the word 'church' stands primarily for the 'visible' group of believers in a particular city or region. In the New Testament the church is, first of all, the church in Rome, in Corinth, in Ephesus or in the region of Galatia.

This is something of crucial importance. Even though the New Testament recognizes that there are ties between churches in different places, and that there must be a sense of unity and solidarity among individual churches; and even though we read of inter-church consultations and of people (in particular the apostles) who travel between the individual congregations and provide support and counsel, *the church was first of all the local church!* I believe this principle is just as valid today. I recognize that religious umbrella organizations are needed, and that structures, and even rules and policies, are inevitable. But that should never lead us to believe that these 'higher' organizations constitute the essence of the church. We must be clear that the Adventist Church does not equal the General Conference structure or the organizational machinery at the division, union and conference levels, and that the most important meeting of church members is not the world congress that is held once every five years. The most important building block of the church is the local congregation of believers and the most important meeting of the church is the worship service on Sabbath morning when a group of believers meets as a congregation to connect with God.

This means that what happens in the church at large may be important and may give many of us great worries, but it should not be our ultimate concern. I must continuously remind myself that my church is not located in Silver Spring, near Washington DC, in the United States of America, and that my church is not in the first place a wonderful, (or not always so wonderful), international organization. *My church is above everything else my local church.*

The international or national umbrella organization of the church is not a divinely ordained creation. Nowhere in the Bible do we read about a General Conference, or about unions and conferences. We do not hear of nominating committees, church manuals or policy books. We read about apostles, pastors and teachers, but not about presidents and departmental directors. All these things that we have in our church's organizational structure are secondary. They are human inventions. The Adventist form of church government is a combination of elements that the early Adventist leaders borrowed from the denominations from which they came. These were gradually further developed on the basis of what was considered useful for keeping the local churches connected, and for assisting them with their mission. Again, this does not mean that I am discounting all forms of organization and that I would want to do away with all 'higher' church levels. But it does mean that I can feel reasonably relaxed when I see and hear things at these various levels that I disagree with.

I am a member of my local church. My first loyalty is to the congregation of which I am a part. Therefore, my priority question is, Can I relate in a meaningful way to my local church? Is my local church a place where I can worship with others and feel spiritually at home? Is there an atmosphere where I can thrive spiritually, emotionally, socially and intellectually? Is it a church where I can think for myself and am allowed to have doubts and to disagree with others? Is it a church where I can contribute with my specific gifts and talents?

WHAT, IF MY CHURCH IS LESS THAN IDEAL?

Some people get lucky. They find a church that fits their needs. But not all are so fortunate and that is where the problem lies for many 'believers on the margins.' Many are fed up with their local church, because they experience intolerance. They find that they cannot ask too many questions, and certainly cannot express any ideas that seem to be in tension with official Adventist teaching. They find few, if any, people with whom they can have a frank discussion about the concerns they have, and they feel that the church services are largely irrelevant to where they are in their everyday life. They have grown tired of rehashing nineteenth century ideas, and of fighting over doctrinal issues. And they cannot stomach people who know everything, because 'the Bible says so,' and because they know exactly how what they read in their Bible must be interpreted. Small wonder that people ask themselves how they can survive in such a church. How can they be expected to (re-)connect with such a congregation, with all its legalism and fundamentalism?

We must recognize that no church—i.e. no congregation—is perfect. This is for the simple reason that it always consists of imperfect human beings. (As soon as people claim to be perfect, all warning bells should start ringing, as trouble and intolerance is never far away.) Recently I read once again the first letter of Paul to the Corinthians. This time it struck me perhaps more than ever before how good it is to read a book of the Bible in its entirety, preferably in one session (although that may not always be feasible for such Bible books as the Psalms or Ezekiel). However, reading 1 Corinthians takes at most only two hours! It is worth the effort.

The apostle had quite a few unpleasant things to say to the church members in Corinth. There were lots of issues that needed to be addressed. The church suffered from serious fragmentation, with several groups claiming their own favorite leader (1:11, 12). But there were also other problems. Paul had heard of immorality in the church of a kind that did not even occur in 'the world,' but had become quite common among the members (5:1). When members of the church had conflicts among themselves they took each other to court (6:1). In addition, there were serious disturbances during the worship services (11) and major deviations with regard to key facets of the Christian faith. Some Corinthian Christians even denied that there would be a resurrection of the dead (15:12).

After I had read the sixteen (mostly short) chapters, I concluded: Fortunately, things are not as bad in most of the local churches that I know, as they were in Corinth! But after reading the entire letter it is good to return to the first chapter, where we read: 'I am writing to God's church in Corinth, to you who have been called by God to be his own holy people... I always thank my God for you and for the gracious gifts he has given you, now that you belong to Christ Jesus. Through him, God has enriched your church in every way—with all of your eloquent words and all of your knowledge' (1:4-9, NLT).

In spite of all the things that were wrong, the people in Corinth were the church of Christ, and Paul was very grateful for them and for the gifts that God had bestowed upon them. Reading this, it seems that we have every reason to remain positive and optimistic about our own local church, and not to despair too quickly, even when there are things we find very difficult to accept! It may be that those of us who have given up on their local church, or are on the verge of doing so, have not focused enough on the good things that can be found in any local congregation. Even in a church with some extreme elements and with a legalistic, fundamentalist undercurrent, usually the nice and theologically more balanced people are in the majority. They often are simply less vocal than the few who feel they have 'the truth.'

However, we must also face the fact that we ourselves are not one hundred percent perfect. We may be impatient and lack sufficient tact. Maybe we have become too accustomed to standing on the sidelines—to being 'on the margins'—and have not tried hard enough to make our own contribution towards a healthy and pleasant church. And it could well be that at times we simply expect too much from our church, and that it may be time to make a concerted effort to get beyond our frustrations—however valid they may seem to us.

WHERE DO I GO?

I realize that for many these arguments may remain hollow and unconvincing. They have tried to be positive with respect to their church; they have endured the negative comments when they asked questions; they have sat through the worship service without feeling spiritually fed. They just cannot go on.

I attend church almost every week. Often I preach myself; at times I listen. When, very occasionally, I skip a service I tend to have mixed feelings. It is nice, especially after a full week, to simply relax with a good book or by taking a brisk walk. But I usually also have a sense that not having participated in a worship service with other people leaves my Sabbath experience incomplete. Yet I must confess that from time to time I visit local churches that leave me wondering, 'If I lived in this town, or in this region of the country, would I want to be here, in this church, every week? If I had no other option but to go to this church, would I be able to endure this experience week after week, month after month?' I admit that I sometimes sympathize with people who have said, 'Enough is enough.'

In times past few people—I am speaking now of my own country—had their own cars and most had to walk to church or were dependent on their bikes or on public transport. It was most convenient to go to the nearest congregation, whatever its size and whatever its composition. Also, in many countries people were used to the 'parish system.' In the state churches, for instance, you were automatically a member of the church in the town or village where you lived. It was hard or even impossible to transfer your membership to a different congregation. In many countries this system was deeply engrained in society and was something people took with them when they became Seventh-day Adventists. Today, this has changed. Most people no longer feel they have to worship in the place where they live. People tend to go 'church shopping' and look for a church where they feel at home. They may even hop across denominational borders. Often their choice of the congregation where they want to belong is not primarily based on the teachings of the church, but rather on the over-all atmosphere, the music, the preaching skills of the pastor, the facilities for the children and easy parking access.

I personally believe that, as a rule, it is better to be part of a congregation that is not too far from where you live. It makes it easier to participate actively in various activities outside of the Sabbath worship. But being part of a congregation in which you cannot breathe, and where you almost feel an alien who has come from another planet, may be too high a price to pay for this geographical nearness. Some Adventist 'believers on the margins' may choose to attend a Sunday church instead. (Or go there in addition to going to church on Sabbath. Someone once told me, 'I go to my church on the Sabbath because that is where I find "the truth," but then I go to another church on Sunday to really worship!) I think I would decide to attend a Sunday church if there were no Sabbath keeping church in the country or within a hundred kilometer or so radius. I would, I think, do this because I have a deep-felt need to worship together with other people. But for me it would, however, be a step of last resort, for I am a committed *Seventh-day* Adventist. And I would urge all Adventists 'on the margins' to connect with an *Adventist* congregation.

If there are options, do some church shopping and see where you fit best, and where your spiritual needs are best catered for. If that means driving past a few other congregations, that would be a lot better than not going to church at all or being part of something that has little or no meaning for you. Considering the fact that nowadays most people have a car and that often there are several churches within driving distance—as is usually the case in areas around major Adventist institutions, or in large cities and in small countries—that would often be feasible. And perhaps there is an innovative church 'plant' or a nearby 'house church' that is worth checking out!

YOU ARE THE CHURCH!

In the previous chapter I pleaded with all of you who are 'believers on the margins' not to give up on God. You need your faith in order to be a whole human being. You may be plagued by doubts and uncertainties, but, at the very least, try to believe. I emphasized that faith is a gift and suggested that in order to receive that gift we do well to spend time in an environment where the language of faith is spoken and the gift of faith is most likely to be distributed. In this chapter I plead with you not to give up on the church.

I do not want to give up on the Seventh-day Adventist denomination and I will continue to plead with Adventist 'believers on the margins' also to stick with Adventism, even when it is at times tempting to leave. In these paragraphs I am specifically making a case for not giving up on your membership in a local church. All of us need the togetherness with others; we need the sacred routine of Sabbath worship. We need the regular experience of sitting at the Lord's table. *We need to belong.*

At the same time we must also bear in mind that *others need us.* They need our input. The people who think they have all the answers must hear our questions. Those who have questions like we have must see and hear that there are others who are also struggling with their faith and their church. It may at times be difficult for 'believers on the margins' to function in a rewarding way in a particular congregation, but part of the problem may be that they, in fact, have failed to leave their own imprint on their church and have contributed very little or nothing to its well-being.

When you do not contribute to a community, you stay, or become, an outsider. On the other hand, when you try to give of yourself—of who you are and what you bring with you in terms of talents and skills—you get involved. The community will benefit from what you bring to it, but you yourself will benefit most. Most 'believers on the margins' have talents and gifts their church needs. True enough, you may not want to function in certain roles, because it might create controversy or force you to suppress or compromise part of who you are. But there are always areas in which you can have a positive, constructive role without sacrificing your integrity.

Some 'believers on the margins' have ceased to contribute financially to their church and are no longer among the 'faithful tithe payers.' Some continue to give money to their church, but channel it to specific projects or to institutions like ADRA—the Adventist Development and Relief Agency. They are willing to give money but they no longer feel inclined to send it to the headquarters office in a particular country or region. They choose to support specific projects, or the work of people they know and appreciate, but do not want to strengthen the organizational system. And most definitely they do not want any of their money to end up in the coffers of the General Conference.

I can understand their reasoning. I myself do continue to give 'through the system,' even though I object to quite a few things I see 'in the system.' It is, however, my personal belief that I have no right to criticize 'a system' and work for change 'in the system,' if I no longer support it by being active and by contributing to its operation. And I find it self-evident that I help to pay for the running of a local church as long as I have ties with that church.

I would urge all 'believers on the margins' to continue to give to their church in some way or other. I will not get into the question as to whether the New Testament requires every believer to give exactly ten percent of his income. I do not believe there is any definitive command or prescription to that effect. It is clearly suggested in the New Testament that it is good to give regularly and generously, and the tithing method seems to be a useful model for that purpose. Ceasing to contribute financially is a way of cutting the umbilical cord that connects you with the church. On the other hand, continuing to give, regardless of the problems you have with your church—as a denomination or as a local church—helps to give or restore a sense of belonging and is a sign of accepting a degree of responsibility for the processes in your church.

When everything is said and done, what I wanted to say in this chapter boils down to just a few points. Your criticism of your (local) church may be very legitimate, and your sense of being an outsider and of being left spiritually dry may be very real. But do not give up on the church. You need it and the church needs you. You must do all you can to find a congregation or group that can provide what you are looking for. But do not over-ask, for congregations will always remain a collective of imperfect human beings. Yet there is also always another dimension. Local churches are also the places where the gift of faith is handed out. Therefore, look for that gift and contribute to the wellbeing and growth of that community. As you do so, you may be able to slowly but surely distance yourself from 'the margins' and enjoy a much richer and far more satisfying relationship with your church—with fellow believers and with your God.

---

1   Jonathan Haidt, *The Righteous Mind* (London, UK: Penguin, 2012), p. 285.

CHAPTER 8

What exactly must I believe?[1]

A t the time when our son was enrolled in the Christian elementary school in the Dutch town where we lived, now over forty years ago, my wife volunteered to help the students in acquiring good reading skills. Her offer was appreciated, but there was a slight problem. The school had an explicit Calvinist identity and required all teachers and volunteers to sign a statement that they agreed with the *Three Forms of Unity*. My wife had never even heard of these 'Three Forms.' Logically, she did not want to sign anything she had never read and, as a result, offered her volunteer services to the adjacent public school.

What are these *Three Forms of Unity?* They concern some documents the Dutch Calvinists of the sixteenth and seventeenth century accepted as authoritative. The best known of these three is the *Heidelberger Catechism.* One of them has to do with the controversy about 'free will' that was raging between the Arminian 'free will' camp and those who advocated fully-fledged predestination. Even though the school administrators indicated that signing the statement was a mere formality, my wife did not like the fact that she was obliged to indicate her agreement with these ancient documents and the doctrinal views that these documents represent. Up until today the 'Three Forms of Unity' belong to the so-called confessional documents of the Protestant Church in the Netherlands (PKN). Does this mean that most of the members of this denomination (and of other denominations in the Calvinist tradition in the Netherlands and elsewhere) know what these documents contain? I am afraid most of them have at best some vague idea. My guess is that the vast majority has never even read one letter of them. But many discussions about certain aspects of these documents have demonstrated that it remains extremely difficult to change even a single paragraph or a few words. This is what tends to happen when a church adopts a 'creed.'

This is precisely what the early leaders of the Adventist Church had in mind when they voiced their opposition to adopting any formal confession of faith. They had seen how, in the denominations in the United States that they were acquainted with, such documents had acquired almost the same level of authority as the Bible, and they had experienced how difficult it was to have an open discussion about even minor aspects of such a creed. Everything had been defined once and for all, and one had to stick to what the wise men of the past had decided. The Adventist pioneers therefore loudly and proudly proclaimed, *'We have no creed but the Bible!'*

But gradually the reluctance to develop a 'creed' dissipated. And today we have a document that is known as the twenty-eight *Fundamental Beliefs of Seventh-day Adventists.* It has become much more than a simple enumeration of the most important Adventist beliefs. The *Fundamental Beliefs* have become a test of orthodoxy. The bottom line is, *This is what you must believe, if you really want to be part of the church.*

Does this mean that all Seventh-day Adventist know more or less what the twenty-eight 'fundamentals' are all about? Far from it. I have at times done a little investigating and concluded that most Dutch Adventists may perhaps be able to list a dozen or so of the 'fundamentals.' And, let's be honest; most newly baptized members do not have a clear idea of the portent of many of these twenty-eight *Beliefs.* In far-away countries the situation is probably not any better. I do not think that most of the 30,000 members who not long ago, after an evangelistic campaign of some weeks, were baptized in Zimbabwe, or that the 100,000 men and women who were baptized in one single evangelistic campaign in Rwanda in May 2016, will be able to name more than a handful of 'fundamental' Adventist beliefs.

Top church leadership was involved with these mass baptisms and praised God for the 'rich harvest of souls.' Yet, at the same time, these church leaders have at various occasions said that you cannot be a good Adventist if you do not fully subscribe to all twenty-eight *Fundamental Beliefs*. It seems that something does not quite add up.

Undeniably, the Adventist statement of the *Fundamental Beliefs* is an important document. Nevertheless, we must not make it more important than it is. The *Fundamental Beliefs* must never acquire the sterile status of a 'confession of faith' that can be used as a checklist to determine a person's orthodoxy (or the lack thereof). That simply is totally at odds with our Adventist tradition.

DO WE NEED DOCTRINES?

Many believers wonder, Do we really need doctrines? And if so, what doctrines are crucial and which might be less essential? In the minds of many believers doctrines or dogmas are associated with theology and with a purely intellectual approach to religion. Why, many would say, is it not enough to have a 'simple' child-like faith? Although faith and doctrine may at times seem to be in tension with each other, they are not opposites but are closely connected and complement each other.

Doctrine—or theology—*results* from faith, but also *nurtures* our faith. Faith, according to the famous statement of medieval theologian St Anselm, 'seeks to understand itself.' This 'seeking to understand' is not just an individual quest for truth, but takes place in the context of a community. The community of believers naturally wants to grasp what it believes, and wants to describe this in some kind of systematic order. It wants to know the implications of its faith, in theory and practice. Most Christians would say that the doctrines they believe in are based on the Bible, but that would be an oversimplification. For reading and studying the Bible does not happen in a vacuum, but always within a community, in a historical context and in a particular culture.

It seems to me that we might compare the role of doctrine in our faith experience with that of grammar in the domain of language. Grammar is not the same as language, but grammar gives structure to language.

Therefore it helps us to make ourselves understood when we explain to other people what we believe. The more skilled we are in our use of the kind of language that is structured by good grammar, the better we will be able to communicate particular concepts to others. This is, in a way, also true for the role of doctrine with respect to faith. We must at least have a basic knowledge of the 'grammar' of the language of faith, if we want to make sense when talking about the content of what we believe.

If we have faith in God—if we trust him and want to connect with him—we naturally also want to know more about him and about his expectations of us. The *who*-dimension (we trust in *Someone*) should always come first, but there must also be a *what* and a *how* to our religion, a dimension of knowing and of acting on that knowledge.

Doctrines are, it is commonly stated, an attempt to translate Truth into human language. This imposes many limitations, even if the Holy Spirit is recognized as a major agent in the process. For it will always remain impossible to express divine concepts adequately in human categories, concepts, symbols, and language. We must never lose sight of this vitally important fact. But, with due recognition of the humanness of our doctrines, they remain essential to give structure to any expression of our faith.

IS EVERYTHING EQUALLY IMPORTANT?

Not all things in life are equally important. We often say, 'The main thing is to be healthy!' Health is usually seen as more important than social status. And, fortunately, most people rate family and friends higher than all sorts of material things. Life becomes very miserable if one does not know how to differentiate between things that are really important and the things that have a lower priority.

The same applies to the sphere of church and spiritual life. The 'higher' church organizations (in the Adventist church: General Conference, divisions, unions, conferences) certainly have an important role to play in the life of the church, but the local church is the place *where the rubber hits the road*. Likewise, a good understanding of theological issues is important, but a close tie with God and a faith that keeps us going in our daily life is much more essential. So, it is also natural to ask whether all Christian doctrines are equally important and whether all *Fundamental Beliefs* of our church are 'fundamental,' i.e. foundational, to the same degree.

Often I hear people say, If something is part of the Truth, we cannot say that it is relatively unimportant or less important than something else. *Truth is Truth!* Who are we to say that a particular truth is not quite as important as another aspect of truth? But, let's be honest; that is not how things really are. Most (in fact, I suspect, all) Adventists intuitively sense that particular points define their being Adventist, while other points do not fall in that same category. For instance, for all of us the Sabbath is (I hope) more important than our abstention from pork.

On May 20, 2004 Albert Mohler Jr, the President of the Southern Baptist Theological Seminary in Louisville, Kentucky, posted an article on his website entitled, 'A Call for Theological Triage and Christian Maturity.'[2] The word *triage* comes from the French word 'to sort' and is mainly used in the medical sphere. In times of war, or when a catastrophe strikes, it must be determined who requires priority medical care. Not all wounds are life threatening, while some are fatal if not treated immediately. In a similar way, Mohler argues, Christians must determine 'a scale of theological urgency,' that is, they must rank doctrines in their order of importance. He suggests that there are 'first-level theological issues' that include doctrines that are 'central and essential to the Christian faith.' Those who deny these doctrines would cease to be Christians. Then, he says, there are second-degree doctrinal issues. They too are important, but in a different way. They mark Christians as belonging to a particular denomination. A total denial of these doctrines would make it difficult, at the very least, to remain within the faith community that sees these doctrines as truly distinctive and as an essential part of its identity. In third place there are theological positions over which even members of one and the same congregation or of a particular denomination may disagree, without jeopardizing their fellowship.

Mohler contends that such a 'triage' is important since it will help us avoid fighting over third-level issues as if they were first-order doctrines, while on the other hand it also sends a strong signal that certain first-order doctrines should not be treated as if they belong to the second or third order. It would seem that this also has significant implications for the way in which a church community proclaims its message, especially in the emphasis particular facets of their teachings receive.

Mohler was not the first person to raise the issue, nor will he be the last. The question as to what are 'essential' or 'first-order' doctrines comes in two forms: (1) What is the core of the Christian faith? (2) What are the *key doctrines* of the church I belong to? When you ask people in various denominations, or in different congregations that are part of the same denomination, what they see as the main aspects of their denominational theology, you will get many different answers. This is also true in the Seventh-day Adventist Church. When asked what are the key Adventist doctrines, church members will usually not cite the entire list of twenty-eight 'fundamental beliefs,' but they will mention just a few—and not always the same ones. This is true for 'believers on the margins' as well as for those Adventists who do not share the same doubts as those who are 'marginal' because of their objections and doubts.

Another important element in our discussion is the fact that the doctrines of a religious tradition are not static but tend to *change* over time. Change in doctrine, or 'development of doctrine' as many prefer to say, has been, and is, a constant feature of the Christian church. If you wonder whether that is true, go to a theological library (or surf on the internet) and you will discover that thousands of books have been written about the history of Christian doctrine and the changes and developments that have taken place. There are different theories about the ways in which doctrinal developments take place.[3] Some argue that later doctrinal developments mostly just clarify earlier Christian teachings, while others identify far more 'real' change.

In the course of their history, Adventists have changed their minds about many things. In the very beginning, the small group of believers that had experienced 'the great disappointment' of 1844 (when Jesus, contrary to their expectations, failed to appear on the clouds of heaven), was convinced that 'the door of grace' had been shut. Christ had left the heavenly sanctuary, they said, and the eternal destiny of all people was sealed. These 'shut door' Adventists—Ellen G. White among them—saw no need to tell people outside of their group about their beliefs, since this could not have any further effect. People were either saved or lost. However, it did not take very long before most of these early 'shut door' Adventist believers changed their minds and began to develop a sense of mission, realizing that others had to be warned of the 'soon' coming of Christ.

Or to mention another example of change: In the early period of Adventism, the role of obedience to God's commandments was so strongly emphasized that the truth of salvation as God's gracious gift was hidden under a thick layer of legalism. I referred earlier to the change in perspective with regard to the doctrine of the Trinity. I could also add that many of the specific predictions that were made on the basis of the traditional Adventist understanding of prophecy had to be corrected as time went by, such as for instance the traditional views on Armageddon at the time of World War I and also around World War II. And so on.[4]

An in-depth analysis of doctrinal change in the course of Adventist history would show that doctrinal change was mainly of a particular type. Adventists changed elements of many of their views, but, once the denomination was firmly established, they did little to initiate new doctrines. As time went by they did, however, see the need to change particular emphases in the way they expressed their doctrinal views, in order to restore balance and to underline their full Christian identity. But even the shifting of emphases does constitute a change, which over time often had a significant impact.[5]

There is no doubt that there has been change in Adventist beliefs and in the manner in which these have been expressed in print and otherwise. This change has often been gradual and seldom assumed the form of a direct denial of a conviction that was previously held. George Knight, an expert on Adventist history, maintains that 'the history of Adventist theology is one of ongoing transformation.'[6] In other words, doctrinal change is not a matter of imagination but has been, and is, real.

Another factor to be noted is the insistence by the Adventist 'pioneers' (Ellen White most definitely among them) on the dynamic nature of 'present truth,' that is recognized in the distinct possibility of 'new light.' In 1892 Ellen G. White wrote:

> ... *Shall we drive our stakes of doctrine one after the other, and then try to make Scripture meet our established opinions? ... Long cherished opinions must not be regarded as infallible ...*
> *We have many lessons to learn, and many, many to unlearn. God and heaven alone are infallible. Those who think they will never have to give up a cherished view, never have occasion to change an opinion, will be disappointed.*[7]

And she expressed herself much in the same way later in this same year:

> *There is no excuse for anyone in taking the position that there is no more truth to be revealed, and that all our expositions of Scripture are without error. The fact that certain doctrines have been held as truth for many years by our people is not a proof that our ideas are infallible. Age will not make error into truth, and truth can afford to be fair. No doctrine will lose anything by close investigation.*[8]

Even today the Adventist Church has (at least in theory) a procedure for studying seriously any 'new light' that might emerge. The facts just mentioned are important to keep in mind as we discuss the matter of differentiating between various levels of doctrinal importance, and they help us not to become overly concerned about the dangers of relativism and subjectivism, as soon as people begin to ask questions about the 'core' of Adventist teachings and advocate some changes.

THE 'PILLARS' OF OUR FAITH

It cannot be denied that Adventists have, from the very beginning of their movement, believed that certain elements of their message were more prominent than others. The 1872 statement of beliefs informed the reader that its intent was to highlight 'the *more prominent features*' of the faith.[9] Ellen White often referred to the 'pillars of truth' and to the 'landmarks' of our faith. Although her application of these terms was rather fluid, it is clear that she did not regard all doctrines as having equal importance.[10]

The fact that Ellen White and other early Adventist leaders differentiated in the importance of individual doctrines was not based on a careful theological analysis, but was prompted by their perception of the church's mission. They were convinced they had to preach the truths that had been obscured by traditional religion and were now being rediscovered. They lived and worked in an environment in which they could safely assume that most of the people they attracted subscribed to the basic Christian teachings of conservative Protestantism. This explains why these common doctrines were not highlighted.

The realization that other elements of the Christian message, which were part of the orthodox Christian tradition, must not be neglected, while the specifically Adventist doctrines were to especially emphasized, emerged only gradually as the denomination further developed. This is also illustrated in the writings of Ellen G. White. As she matured in her thinking her emphases shifted significantly. A quote from 1893 may serve as a good illustration: 'Christ and his character and work, is the *center* and circumference of all truth, He is the chain upon which the jewels of doctrine are linked.'[11] This is not the kind of statement she would have made in the early years of her ministry.

The idea that perhaps not all of the twenty-eight *Fundamental Beliefs* carry equal weight seems to be confirmed by the fact that the statement of 'commitment,' to which baptismal candidates are expected to give their assent, offers a summary of just thirteen doctrines, which are expressed much more succinctly than in the corresponding formulation of these particular doctrines in the statement of *Fundamental Beliefs*. The thirteen-point *Baptismal Vow* closely reflects this statement of commitment. Interestingly, a much shorter 'alternative vow' is also considered acceptable. This alternative vow contains a reference to 'the teachings of the Bible as expressed in the Statement of Fundamental Beliefs,' whereas in the regular vow no such reference is deemed necessary, even though it is not as complete as the full text of the twenty-eight Fundamentals.[12] Should the list to which baptismal candidates give their assent perhaps be considered as more 'fundamental' than 'the twenty-eight'?

The opinions of church members regarding the statement of *Fundamental Beliefs* vary widely. One can find church members who hold a very 'high' view of the *Fundamental Beliefs* and regard each line, or even each word, as semi-inspired. It is an attitude that borders on what one might call 'fundamentolatry.'[13] On the other hand there is, I believe, a widespread sentiment that the statement of the *Fundamental Beliefs* is far too detailed and strangely mixes life style standards with doctrinal issues.[14]

If it is a valid premise that some doctrines are more important than others, how then can we get beyond our individual preferences when we try to do our 'triage'? Can we establish sound criteria by which we may establish a 'hierarchy' of doctrine in Adventist theology?

Whatever model we develop, one underlying fact is clearly provided by Scripture in a statement of Christ himself. We read in John 14:6 that *Christ declared that he is the Truth,* i.e. that all Truth radiates from him. Every doctrine that claims to be 'truth' must therefore relate to the person and work of Jesus Christ. *Christ is the center and he must be the foundation of any truly Christian 'system' of 'fundamental' truths.* This is what the gospel—the 'good news'—is all about. 'It is the power of God for the salvation of everyone who believes' (Romans 1:16). 'Salvation is found in no one else,' but in Christ (Acts 4:12). Acceptance or denial of this 'fundamental' truth determines whether one is in God's camp or not. We may quote another word from Christ's own lips that confirms this: 'Whoever believes in the Son has eternal life. But whoever rejects the Son will not see life, for God's wrath remains on him' (John 3:36). The 'knowledge of our Lord Jesus Christ' is crucial, and believers must make sure that it is not 'ineffective and unproductive' (2 Peter 1:8). John uses even stronger language: Everyone 'who denies that Jesus is the Christ' is labeled 'antichrist' (1 John 2:22). George Knight underlines the importance of this point of departure by stating that 'a relationship with Jesus and an understanding of the cross of Christ and other central elements of the plan of salvation informs a person's understanding of doctrine.'[15] Having made this crucial point, how do we proceed further?

TWO, THREE, FOUR LAYERS?

The first question that the book *Seventh-day Adventists Answer Questions on Doctrine* deals with is, 'What doctrines do Seventh-day Adventists hold in common with Christians in general, and in what aspects of Christian thought do they differ?' In the reply three categories of doctrines are distinguished:

1. doctrines Adventists have 'in common with conservative Christians and the historic Protestant creeds';
2. 'certain controverted doctrines that we share with some but not with all conservative Christians'; and
3. 'a few doctrines [that] are distinctive with us.'[16]

The total number of doctrines listed in these three categories is thirty-six. This reminds us of Albert Mohler, whom we met earlier in this chapter, and who, likewise, suggested three different doctrinal layers. Other authors have suggested a similar two- or three-layered approach to doctrine.[17]

This type of classification may be helpful to clarify what is, and what is not, unique to the community to which one confesses to belong, but it does not offer us any direct assistance for determining which Adventist doctrines are more fundamental than others. The adaptation offered by Woodrow Whidden may be useful in taking us a step forward.[18] He suggests that we must distinguish between doctrines that reflect the common orthodox Christian heritage from those that are 'Adventist.' Whidden further suggests that there are *Adventist* doctrines that may be called 'essential': those elements that form the 'essential framework of Adventist theological discourse.' He further suggests that some Adventist doctrines may be considered as 'non-essential.'[19] George Knight, in contrast to Whidden, is of the opinion that life style issues must also fit somewhere into this classification of truth.[20]

I would like to propose a model in which these various elements are combined. I am certainly not suggesting this is the last word on the issue, but it has helped me to get a firmer handle on the question of what is more and what is less important for my spiritual journey. Graphically it would look like a few circles:

Let me venture to suggest some examples of doctrines and views for each category.

In category (1) I would place, for example: God as Trinity; the triune God as Creator and Sustainer of the universe; salvation and eternal life and judgment through Jesus Christ; the active presence of the Holy Spirit; the inspiration of the Scriptures; a revealed moral code; the main elements of the process of salvation; and a call to preach the gospel.

In category (2) a number of Adventist 'essentials' would find their place, such as the seventh-day Sabbath, the 'soon' return of Christ, baptism by immersion, the importance of the Lord's Supper, the belief in Christ's high priestly ministry, man's call to be stewards, death as a kind of unconscious 'sleep,' and the continuation of spiritual gifts.

Category (3) would, in my view, be the realm of such things as the Adventist philosophy of prophetic interpretation, tithing, dietary instructions, the time aspect of Christ's high priestly ministry ('1844'), and, possibly, the rite of foot washing.

In the last concentric circle (4) I would tend to locate certain specific prophetic interpretations, controversial issues surrounding the inspiration of Ellen White, the never-ending discussion of what is allowed or not allowed on the Sabbath, styles of worship, the specifics about the wearing of 'jewelry,' etc.

See illustration below.

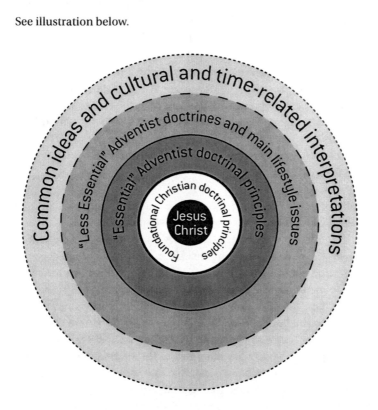

I realize that many Adventists will not be happy with such a model. Some will probably be totally opposed to it, or will react even more strongly. I recognize, in particular, that mentioning examples of what may be placed in each category could prove to be an extremely hazardous exercise in view of my role in the church. But I believe there are many in the church who would welcome a discussion about this topic and who long for an honest debate about what truly belongs to the core of Adventism and what is not 'essential' in quite the same way.

SOME IMPLICATIONS

In a discussion about the ranking of our doctrines a few things must, I believe, be kept in mind. Firstly, I want to re-emphasize that all doctrinal statements must in some way clearly relate to the Center, Jesus Christ. Doctrinal *truth* only becomes *Truth* when it is connected with the person and work of our Lord Jesus Christ.

Secondly, the lines between the categories will not always be totally clear. For that reason I have drawn some dotted lines. The crucial question is, Can we point to a few key doctrines that, without any doubt, solidly belong in each category? 'Believers on the margins' are especially interested in a convincing answer to that question. I would suggest that if there is a 'core' of beliefs, these doctrines would be part of the first two categories.

Thirdly, I have very intentionally separated the foundational *Christian* doctrines from Adventist 'essential' doctrines, although they are in many ways interrelated. It is, for instance, not helpful to compare the relative weight of the Sabbath with that of the doctrine of the Trinity, and then ask which of the two is most important. It would in many ways be a matter of comparing apples with pears. The Seventh-day Adventist identity is determined by a firm commitment to both doctrinal categories. The fact that we are *Christians* first, and, as Christians, have also chosen to be *Adventists,* makes us *Adventist Christians.*[21] Giving primary attention to the foundational *Christian* elements will be a constant reminder that in our day and age we cannot take it for granted that people bring knowledge of these doctrines along when they begin to consider the *Adventist* version of Christianity.

Fourthly, the label 'less essential' means exactly that. It should not be understood as 'unimportant.' Admittedly, any process of classifying doctrine is a subjective undertaking. Mistakes can be made. But it is not *totally* subjective and is not necessarily a sure recipe for disaster. There is guidance through the inspired Word and through the living Spirit. Moreover, we need to remember that, as long as we are imperfect humans, *all* theological activity will remain subjective and, in a sense, risky. But it is not something we should regard as too dangerous and as leading to a moribund 'slippery slope.' In any case, using the 'slippery slope' argument is usually rather a sign of weakness than of principle and clear thinking.

Fifthly, it took Adventists more than a century to arrive at the current summary of our *Fundamental Beliefs*. Doctrinal developments take time. Therefore, it is not to be expected that arriving at a consensus of what constitutes the core of Adventist beliefs, can happen overnight. It will require patience... and tolerance!

Sixthly, I am firmly convinced that, when any further revision of the *Fundamental Beliefs* takes place, the document should not be further extended and become even more detailed, but should rather be shortened. I would welcome a new text that is limited to doctrines that are 'foundational Christian' and 'essential Adventist.' In this connection the words of Robert Greer are worth quoting:

> ... *doctrinal statements ... should not be too comprehensive. When a doctrinal statement is too comprehensive, it (a) runs the risk of becoming dangerously seductive, since it offers a finality of Christian thought that for some people is attractive and comforting; (b) eliminates the need to think critically; (c) mutes the Holy Spirit, who may wish to speak afresh from Scripture to a given individual or community; and (d) breeds triumphalism, which discourages rather than encourages theological conversation across denominational or ecclesiastical boundaries.*[22]

LIBERAL OR CONSERVATIVE?
Almost inevitably, the labels of 'liberalism and 'conservatism' pop up in a discussion about the 'weight' of particular doctrines. Corresponding tags are the even worse sounding terms 'left wing' and 'right wing.' I wish we could avoid these words altogether, since they are very imprecise and tend to be loaded with prejudice or condemnation. To be called a 'liberal' has damaged the career of many a pastor and theology teacher, or worse. On the other hand, being known as a 'conservative' has closed some doors (and pulpits)

for others. Some protest when they are called a 'liberal,' while others are proud of their 'left wing' reputation. Some students, who want to become a pastor, will very intentionally choose a college or university with theology professors who are known to be conservative, while for others this would be a strong incentive to avoid such a college.

What the Bible says about our relationship to others has a direct bearing on the unfortunate polarization between liberals and conservatives. We must love our 'neighbor' as ourselves—for someone who is conservative that must most definitely also include his liberal fellow-believers, and for someone who belongs to the 'left wing' of the church it must include those who are on the 'right wing.' Unfortunately, liberals and conservatives often find it difficult to relate to each other in a pleasant and constructive way, and they hardly listen to each other (and this is true for both parties). Also, in many cases people fail to see that the picture is usually not quite as simple as they imagine, because people are seldom totally liberal or one hundred percent conservative. They may be liberal with respect to some issues, but surprisingly conservative with regards to many other things. We may meet people who are very liberal in their theology, but quite conservative in their life style, and vice versa. I have talked with several young men who feverishly cling to traditional Adventism as far as the teachings of the church are concerned, but then tell me that they are happily cohabiting with their girlfriend!

Alden Thompson, an Adventist theology professor at Walla Walla University (Walla Walla, Washington State), points to three different 'flavors' with regard to liberals and conservatives. What he says does not explain everything, but it definitely strikes a chord with me. Liberals, Thompson says, *love questions, while conservatives want answers.* When it comes to life style, one might say that conservatives love the isolation of the hills, while liberals run to the city to be with people. Conservatives experience God as a powerful presence, while for the liberals God tends to be a more distant reality.[23]

Adventist scholar Fritz Guy tries to summarize his views about conservatism and liberalism in these words: *'Conservatives are* concerned above all to maintain those truths that we already possess, embodied in a gradation we have learned to trust; and, on the other hand, liberals want to seek new truths, or new interpretations of old truths.[24] Well, if that is a correct definition of being a liberal, I will proudly accept that label as an honorary title. It could, however, be argued that the term 'progressive' is to be preferred over the qualification of being a 'liberal.' Professor Guy suggests that most of us indeed tend to be 'liberal' or 'conservative,' but that we can become 'progressive' if we learn from each other, listen more intently to each other and try to grow together.[25]

FUNDAMENTALISM

Another word pair is probably at least as significant when we discuss the diversity in doctrinal opinion, namely *fundamentalism* versus *relativism.* The Christian faith becomes meaningless if we support total relativism, when nothing is certain and no values or ideals demands our total loyalty. As we argued earlier, we do not have hard 'proofs' for the existence of the God we meet in the Bible and who has further revealed himself in Jesus Christ. However, we have enough evidence to take the 'leap' of faith and to accept the implications of this faith. We also referred to the negative aspects of fundamentalism. At this point in our discussion I want to underline these once more, since Adventist conservatism tends (at the very least) to flirt with fundamentalism.

'Fundamentalism—religious and secular—is itself inspired more by doubt than by confidence, more by fear than by quiet faith and settled conviction.'[26] This statement was made by James Davison Hunter (b. 1955), a prominent American sociologist, who contributed much to the popularization of the term 'culture wars.' Hunter argues that fundamentalism is mostly negative. *It rejects what it considers dangerous and reacts primarily to threats.*[27] 'For the fundamentalist it is far easier to target enemies outside the tradition than to seek answers within... It offers no constructive proposals for the everyday problems that trouble most people, and it provides no vital solutions to the problems of pluralism and change. Indeed, just the opposite.'[28]

These are words to remember when we think of the current debates in the Adventist Church. The traditionalists (or fundamentalists, conservatives, 'right wingers,' or whatever terms one might use) tend to be reactive, to be always on the defense, constantly warning against the dangers they see or imagine. They do not like to hear too many questions, certainly not from the 'believers on the margins,' but claim to have all the answers already.

WHO ARE 'REAL' ADVENTISTS?

The *official* answer to the question who may be considered 'real' Adventists would have to be, Those who affirm all twenty-eight *Fundamental Beliefs*. But if that reply is correct, it would exclude most, if not all, 'believers on the margins.' And, yes, if full agreement with all details of these beliefs is required, in the way in which they are currently formulated, I would have to say that I am not a 'real' Adventist. Should that keep me from sleeping soundly? No, it shouldn't.

I do not need to worry unduly about my membership in the Seventh-day Adventist Church (at least as long as I am 'straight' and not 'gay'). If the leaders of the General Conference conclude that I have too many heretical ideas to call myself a genuine Adventist, or even if the leadership of the Netherlands Union has serious problems with some of the things I am saying or writing, they can plead with me to change my opinions, or they may decide not to invite me any longer to preach or to attend certain meetings. They may refuse to endorse and promote any further publications that I may write in the future. They may decide to pray for me, or may even wring their hands in desperation. They may be able to do all that, but they cannot touch my church membership.

Only my local church can vote to accept me as a member or to disfellowship me. However, it is not very likely that they will review my membership any time soon, unless I suddenly begin to show extreme immoral behavior or become disruptive in the worship services. Therefore, 'believers on the margins' can be at ease; as long as the local church where they hold their membership is happy to retain their name on its registry, they are a *bona fide* member of the church. Moreover, most local churches are quite reluctant to sever the ties with people—even with those 'on the margins'—who have not themselves indicated that they want their membership to be cancelled. (And even then it sometimes is not so easy to have one's name removed from the books!)

But let us not just look at this from an administrative angle, as if church membership is only a matter of having one's name on a membership list. Not everyone qualifies to be on this list. If someone wants to be referred to as a 'Christian' he must, I believe, affirm a number of basic Christian principles. It seems to me that a person loses the right to call himself a Christian if he no longer believes in God and in Jesus Christ as someone who plays a decisive role in the relationship between God and humankind. Likewise, I believe that I must share some key Adventist convictions with my fellow Adventist believers if I want to call myself a Seventh-day Adventist. At this point it is important to have a clear idea of what is really 'essential' and 'less essential' in our Adventist teachings.

Whether I am a *true* Adventist is, in final analysis, something I decide myself. I am the one who must determine whether I affirm the basics of the Christian faith and whether I have sufficient affinity with the Adventist interpretation of the Christian faith and with the Adventist faith community, to refer to myself as a 'genuine' Adventist. On that basis I have no hesitation whatsoever in calling myself a 'real' Adventist. And I believe this would be true for most of my fellow church members, including those who see themselves as 'believers on the margins.'

I agree wholeheartedly with Professor Fritz Guy—the theologian I referred to earlier—when he listed a few key aspects of authentic Adventism.[29] He tops his short list with 'having a spirit of openness to present truth.' This means that a genuine Adventist never believes he has all of 'the truth.' Like the earliest Adventist thought leaders, a 'real' Adventist must be willing to change his mind when needed, to continue learning, and growing in his understanding of what it means to be an Adventist Christian in today's world (and not what it meant in the nineteenth century).

We are genuine Adventists, Guy affirms, when we are Christians who have 'God's comprehensive and universal love at the center of our personal existence.' To be worthy of the name 'Seventh-day Adventist' we must appreciate the 'contemporary importance of the Sabbath' and have 'the hopeful anticipation of the reappearance of God in the person of Jesus the Messiah.' Two other important elements that are cited by Guy, are 'the idea of multidimensional human wholeness' and 'the choice of the Adventist community as a spiritual home, with the adoption of the Adventist past as part of one's spiritual identity.'

Many 'believers on the margins' would feel comfortable with Guy's description of an authentic Adventist. I, for one, would consider those who fit Guy's description as 'true' Adventists, regardless of the many doubts they may have. I would challenge myself and all those who have read this chapter, *Let us dare to be, and remain, part of the Adventist faith community, while always thinking independently and never jeopardizing our personal integrity.*

---

1   This chapter contains material that was published in my weekly blogs (www. reinderbruinsma.com) of July 31, August 6, and August 13, 2015, and in a chapter that I wrote for a Festschrift for Dr Jon Dybdahl: 'Are all truths Truth? Some Thoughts on the Classification of Beliefs,' in: Rudi Maier, ed., *Encountering God in Life and Mission—A Festschrift Honoring Jon Dybdahl* (Berrien Springs, MI: Department of World Mission, Andrews University, 2010), pp. 173-188.

2   Albert Mohler, 'A Call for Theological Triage and Christian Maturity,' http://www. albertmohler.com/commentary_read.php?cdate=2004-05-20.

3   See Rolf J. Pöhler, *Continuity and Change in Christian Doctrine* (Frankfurt am Main: Peter Lang (Germany), 1999.

4   Fritz Guy, *Thinking Theologically: Adventist Christianity and the Interpretation of Faith* (Berrien Springs, MI: Andrews University Press, 1999), p. 87.

5   Among early authors who went to great lengths to provide historical credentials for 'new' Adventist doctrinal insights were John N. Andrews and Uriah Smith with their well-researched books on the Sabbath (Andrews) and on conditional immortality (Smith). Later, LeRoy E. Froom left as his *magnum opus* his 4-volume *Prophetic Faith of our Fathers*, which attempted to show how the 'new' prophetic understandings of Adventism were mainly rediscoveries of interpretations that were held by many theologians and church leaders in previous centuries. This, he maintained, was also true of the Adventist rediscovery of a number of foundational Christian doctrines, such as the Trinity, and the full deity and eternity of Christ, to which he referred as the 'eternal verities.' The publication of the rather controversial book *Seventh-day Adventists Answer Questions on Doctrine* in 1953 offers further proof of the felt need to clarify some Adventist beliefs and to show that these beliefs, in fact, conformed to orthodox Christian dogma. Even today, however, many believe that this book did much more than this, i.e. that it signified a real substantial dogmatic reorientation.

6   George R. Knight, *A Search for Identity: The Development of Seventh-day Adventist Beliefs* (Hagerstown, MD: Review and Herald, 2000), p. 12.

7   Ellen G. White, *Counsels to Writers and Editors* (Nashville, TN: Southern Publishing Association, 1946), pp. 36, 37.

8   Ellen G. White, *Advent Review and Sabbath Herald*, 20 December 1892.

9   Gary Land, *Adventism in America* (Grand Rapids, MI: Wm. B. Eerdmans, 1986), p. 231.

10 See Reinder Bruinsma, 'Are all truths Truth? Some Thoughts on the Classification of Beliefs,' p. 180, where quotes are provided from various Ellen G. White sources: *Selected Messages*, vol. 2, pp. 104-107; *Counsels to Writers and Editors*, 1946, pp. 29-31, *The Great Controversy*, 1911, p. 409; See also Ellen G. White, *Manuscript 24*, November or December 1888, quoted in: George R. Knight, *From 1888 to Apostasy: The Case of A.T. Jones* (Hagerstown, MD: Review and Herald, 1987), p. 40.

11 Eric Claude Webster, *Crosscurrents in Adventist Theology* (Berrien Springs, MI: Andrews University Press, 1984), p. 150.

12 See *Church Manual*, 2015, pp. 45, 46.

13 A neologism inspired by the term bibliolatry that refers to worship of the Scriptures.

14 Bryan W. Ball, 'Towards an Authentic Adventist Identity,' in: B. Schantz and R. Bruinsma, eds., *Exploring the Frontiers of Faith—Festschrift for Jan Paulsen* (Lüneburg, Germany: Saatkorn Verlag, 2009), p. 67.

15 George R. Knight, 'Twenty-seven Fundamentals in Search of a Theology,' *Ministry*, February 2001), pp. 5-7.

16 George R. Knight, ed., *Seventh-day Adventists Answer Questions on Doctrine*, annotated edition, pp. 21-24.

17 See e.g. Robert C. Greer in his widely acclaimed book *Mapping Postmodernism: A Survey of Christian Options* (Downers Grove. IL: InterVarsity Press, 2003), pp. 172ff.

18 Woodrow II Whidden, *Ellen White on the Humanity of Christ* (Hagerstown, MD: Review and Herald, 1997), pp. 77-88.

19 Ibid, p. 80.

20 George R. Knight, 'Twenty-seven Fundamentals in Search of a Theology,' pp. 5-7.

21 Bryan W. Ball, op. cit., p. 58.

22 Robert C. Greer, op. cit., p. 174.

23 Alden Thompson, *Beyond Common Ground: Why Liberals and Conservatives Need Each Other* (Nampa, ID: Pacific Press, 2009), p. 121.

24 'Fritz Guy, *op. cit.*, p. 27.
25 Ibid., p. 29.
26 James Davison Hunter, 'Fundamentalism and Relativism Together': Reflections on Genealogy,' pp. 17-34, in: Peter L. Berger, ed. *Between Relativism and Fundamentalism: Religious Resources for a Middle Position* (Grand Rapids, MI: Wm. B. Eerdmans, 2010), p. 34.
27 Ibid., p. 32.
28 Ibid., p. 33.
29 Fritz Guy, op. cit., p. 92.

CHAPTER 9

Dealing with our doubts

I n this last chapter I will try to pull things together. We began our discussion in the first few chapters by surveying the state of the Christian church in the Western world. We concluded that the church is in crisis and also saw how millions of men and women in the West are experiencing a crisis in their faith. Many even doubt the existence of an almighty and loving God. For a large group this doubt also affects a range of other things they used to believe in. They realize that some important traditional teachings of their church no longer find an echo in their soul. Then we focused in particular on the Seventh-day Adventist Church. We noted that large numbers of people have left the church, and that many others are near the exit. They see trends in their church that they cannot live with and they wonder whether some of the traditional doctrines of the church can still be relevant for their everyday life. I have referred to this large group of people, who are unhappy with their church and who experience lots of doubts regarding the content of their faith, as 'believers on the margins.'

In later chapters I have attempted to encourage those of you who are 'on the margins' to take a (new) 'leap' of faith. I have shared my conviction that, even though we may not have absolute proof that God exists and cares for us, we have enough reason for the 'wager' of taking this 'leap.' I have tried to encourage you not to give up on the church, but to focus on a local congregation, where you can be yourself, and to remain part of it, or to return to it. In the previous chapter I have begun to suggest a way of dealing with doctrinal doubts. I have argued that being a 'real' Adventist does not require that we will slavishly say 'yea and amen' to all the *Fundamental Beliefs* of our church. I know that this point of view will be heavily criticized by many church leaders as well as by lots of members in the pew. But I am convinced that it creates space in the hearts and minds of many 'believers on the margins,' who feel they are suffocated by the rigidity of some of the traditional doctrines, which no longer relate in any meaningful way to their daily lives.

This is where we pick up the thread in this final chapter. We are not going to discuss individual doctrines in detail, but will look at some more general approaches that may be useful in dealing with our doubts and uncertainties. I am not naive and will not say that all doubts will suddenly dissipate if we read more diligently in our Bible and pray more intensely than before. That is not to say that these two aspects are not essential. They are, in fact, of paramount importance when we try to deal constructively with our doubts.

A SPIRITUAL APPROACH

If we are in doubt as to what kind and color of car we will buy, or whether or not we will follow a particular strategy in the running of our business, there may be some non-rational, or even emotional, factors involved. This type of doubt, however, must basically be dealt with through rational arguments. What size car can I afford? What color do I like, or will please my partner, and what would be the best from the perspective of safety? Will I do well to take out a major loan from the bank to expand my business, or will this be too risky in view of the current economic climate and the fierce competition I am facing?

In dealing with our doubts in the spiritual realm we cannot shift our brain into neutral and merely follow our emotions and feelings. But our intuitions, our feelings and emotions will play a major role. We can only hope to get a handle on our doubts if we allow ourselves to be touched by the Spirit. Our approach to our doubts may perhaps best be summarized by listing five aspects: (1) reading; (2) thinking; (3) praying; (4) talking with others and (5) patience.

As we start on this path we must begin with what we called our 'leap of faith.' This may sound naive, but it's the only option. We must be willing to let ourselves be drawn into the sphere of faith. We must 'try to believe,' as Nathan Brown told us in his little book with this title (to which I referred in Chapter 2). If I have a serious health condition, and have long been searching in vain for the right kind of remedy, I might take a 'leap of faith' and consider visiting a practitioner of alternative medicine and take the medication he prescribes—even though I am not really sure this is going to help. This kind of comparison is, of course, inadequate, but I believe it does tell us something. It is worth trying everything when we are in a quandary. Therefore, read the Bible, pray and go to church—even if you are not yet sure that this will bring you any answers and the kind of inner rest and certainty you are looking for.

READING THE BIBLE

Adventists like to talk (or even boast) about *studying* the Bible. New members usually go through a process of Bible 'studies' to become acquainted with the 'truth.' We have our weekly Bible studies in the so-called Sabbath School. Early Adventism borrowed the Sunday School model from other denominations and adapted it, as time went by, to its specific needs. The institution of the Sabbath School has certainly helped in strengthening biblical literacy among the church members. But more and more Adventists are beginning to realize that this type of Bible 'study' often leaves much to be desired. Most of the quarterly 'study guides' are of a topical nature. A particular theme is selected, and then broken down into thirteen sub-themes. The author of the study guide selects a number of Bible texts that he feels say something about these themes, together with some quotations (usually from Ellen G. White) and some further explanatory comments. Very often the Bible texts are drawn together without much regard for context. The weekly Sabbath School study shows that the traditional proof-text method is still very much alive. And even when during a quarter a particular book of the Bible is studied, relatively little attention tends to be paid to its background, context and particular theology.

I have come to the conclusion that we should perhaps stop *studying* the Bible, and start *reading* the Bible—as a story that we want to follow from the beginning to the end. When we read a novel and enjoy the plot, we will not just select a paragraph here and there and combine these bits and pieces in a random kind of order. If we read a good book, we will want to follow the entire plot and are eager to know how it ends. In a way this also applies to the Bible. It is God's story about his interaction with us and with the world. We do well to read it from beginning to end. We may perhaps skip a few pages (for instance the long genealogies) here and there (as we sometimes also do with ordinary books), but we will want to follow the story line. And the same is true for the separate sections of the Bible we usually refer to as the Bible 'books.' We will only get the full benefit from our reading if we read these sections in their entirety. And some are so short that we can easily read them in one sitting.

When we use this method, we may find that certain well-known texts do not actually say what we always thought they said. When read in isolation from their context we may come to a conclusion that is not warranted when we also read what precedes and follows the text. Even if we do not understand many of the things we come across, we still benefit from our reading by catching the over-all message of the Bible or a part thereof. Consulting books about the Bible, such as a good commentary, is certainly useful but it cannot take the place of the reading of the Bible itself. Unfortunately many Christians read more *about* the Bible than *in* the Bible.

COUNTING THE POTATOES

The Bible contains many unusual stories, but we should not worry too much about this 'strangeness.' Maybe we should expect this in stories that should be read 'freshly and truthfully from one generation to another.'[1] As we read 'we develop some impression of a larger story behind the many smaller stories.'[2] Nathan Brown, from whose book I just quoted, challenges the 'believers on the margins' not to focus too much on the historicity of the biblical stories—the perennial question whether or not the events in the Bible did actually happen in the precise way they have been recorded and transmitted. He suggests that for the time being we 'suspend our unbelief' and engage with the biblical stories as we would with a good novel or movie. 'Choose not to be distracted by the arguments whether the story is true, whether the history can be verified, whether contemporary scientific conclusions can accept such a story. Instead begin to read them to discover the goodness, beauty, wisdom and truth they offer in themselves, as stories.'[3]

Seventh-day Adventists have been told how important it is to 'study' the book of Revelation. For most this usually means reading it piecemeal, text by text or paragraph by paragraph, and consulting one or more of the Adventist commentaries that have been written to help us understand the unusual symbols and to apply the content of John's prophecies to historical events in past, present and future. I have become more and more convinced that this is not the most fruitful approach—and certainly not when one comes to the Revelation for the first time.

Occasionally I do some presentations about the Revelation and nowadays I start these with showing a slide of a painting by Vincent van Gogh (1853-1890)—a famous Dutch impressionist painter. I ask my audience to look intently at this painting of the 'Potato Eaters.' It is a dark, gloomy scene with five people sitting around a table, with an oil lamp swinging from the ceiling. They are eating from one single dish of potatoes. After my audience has been able to look at the painting for a minute or two, I turn the projector off and ask them a few questions about the details of the painting. I ask them, for instance, how many coffee cups they counted and how many potatoes they saw in the bowl on the table. I never get the right answer. That is not what the people have been focusing on. 'So what did you see then?' I ask them. They usually say they saw sadness, gloominess, and, especially, poverty! That is the central message of the painting, rather than providing information about the number of potatoes or the number of coffee cups.

At that point I challenge my audience to read the book of Revelation, preferably several times, from beginning to end. I urge them not 'to count the potatoes,' but to look for the overall message. At some later stage they may get so interested in the subject that they will also want to know the number of potatoes in the bowl and the number of coffee

The Potato Eaters, Vincent van Gogh (1853-1890).

cups on the table. When they have read all twenty-two chapters of the Revelation, without worrying about what a 'seal,' a 'trumpet,' and 'the beast from the sea, and 'the beast from the earth,' et cetera, mean, and have tried to absorb the overall story line and its meaning, they are usually amazed by what they have learned. They see in this unusual section of the Bible how there is, apparently, a dimension that might be described as 'other-worldly,' behind our life and behind the events that happen on this planet. There is much more going on than meets our eye. The people who have chosen to be on God's side in his battle with evil are going through tough times, but somehow they always come through. God's enemies are the losers! The redeemed must exercise patience, but in the end those who remain loyal to God will be safe, i.e. they will be saved. The book of Revelation begins with a vision of Christ walking amidst his churches, while keeping the leaders of these churches in his hands (1:12-20). And it ends in a new world of peace and harmony, where God lives among his people. That is the message that jumps at us when we simply read the entire book and let it speak to us. When we do this we will discover that through the human words of the Bible writers God's Word comes to us.

When we read the Bible to feed our soul—and not primarily to gather information—we find that many of the difficulties that cause us to doubt the Bible largely disappear or become less threatening. Take the book of Jonah as an example. Read the four chapters—this will not take more than half an hour. Do not 'count the potatoes.' Just forget (at least for the time being) about Jonah's three-day stay in the belly of the big fish, and the bush that gave him shade and grew as miraculously as it disappeared again. And do not worry about some of the details of the conversion story of the Ninevites that even included the animals! Just read the story and try to discover what these few chapters tell you. If we do that we see how Jonah tries to escape from God, but without success. It is a story about missions and not about a fish that swallows people. We learn how God has called his prophet for a specific assignment and does not give up on Jonah, when he is unwilling to preach among Israel's archenemies. And note how, later on in the story, Jonah is much more concerned about his own reputation as a prophet than about the salvation of the people of Nineveh. It is a story that has a very direct application to our own life and our relationship with God.

I could cite other examples of parts of the Bible that seem odd, to say the least, but that have a clear message when read in their entirety with a desire to find something that nurtures our soul. As we read we must always be aware that we come to the Bible as a whole, or to any 'book' of the Bible, with a set of presuppositions. We read the Bible through our own lenses. I cannot read the Bible in a purely objective way, however much I try. The home where I grew up, my education, my culture and my personal history 'color' the way in which I read. People in the Western world do not read their Bible in the same way as people read it in the developing world. Urban people have a lens that differs from that of people who live in an agricultural setting. Rich people and poor people do not read in the same way. Many rich people tend to have a special interest in Bible texts that tell them it is all right to be rich. Poor people tend to focus on texts that demand justice and fairness. Bible readers in the Western world see many things in Scripture that seem to support their way of life, while people who live under an oppressive regime are immediately struck by the stories of liberation and freedom.

I have heard Adventists say, I do not understand why people continue to see Sunday as the day of rest, because it is so clear from the Bible that we should keep the seventh-day Sabbath. But remember; *it is clear to us* because for us the Sabbath texts stand out as we read the Bible wearing our Adventist spectacles! Other people do not wear these same spectacles and hardly notice these Sabbath texts, because they simply assume that the day on which Christ was resurrected has replaced the Old Testament Sabbath. Unfortunately, this is how almost all of us read the Bible. As Adventists we immediately highlight the texts that support our doctrinal positions and we automatically tend to ignore or downplay texts that seem not to fit with those convictions. Adventists do not have to feel too guilty about this, for it is a general phenomenon that people filter what they read through the lens of their preconceived ideas.

The first step in our Bible reading is, therefore, that we are aware of the fact that we read though our own personal lenses—and that others do the same. Some time ago someone recommended a small book to me that I found extremely illuminating. It is called *Reading the Bible from the Margins,* and was written by Miguel A. De La Torre, a Cuban-American theologian.[4] De La Torre 'shows how the "standard" readings of the Bible are not always acceptable to people or groups in the "margins". The poor and those who are targets of discrimination because of their ethnic group or gender may have quite different insights and understandings of biblical texts that can be of value to all readers.'[5] As I was writing these paragraphs, it occurred to me that 'believers on the margins' also read the Bible through their own glasses. They may, however, as they read be touched by the Spirit, who inspired the Bible, in ways that escape most of their fellow brothers and sisters.

THINKING

A vital element of dealing with doubt is clear thinking. One important principle of biblical interpretation is the use of common sense. When reading the Bible, after taking the 'leap of faith,' we should not shy away from some hard intellectual work. But through it all we do well to apply common sense. Faith is not just a leap in the dark, contrary to reason and to all evidence. 'Faith seeks understanding,' St Anselm told us. Os Guinness formulates it in these words: 'A Christian is a person who thinks, but believes while he does his thinking.'[6] It is essential not to separate believing from thinking.

Fritz Guy tells us that 'tripolar thinking' is necessary. By this he means that there are three aspects that must be taken into account when we try to understand what the Bible tells us. The three principles that must guide us, and must be kept in balance, are: (1) the Christian gospel, (2) the cultural context and (3) the Adventist heritage.[7] The good news of Jesus Christ must always be at the center of our thinking. Whatever we read in the Bible must always be 'digested' in the light of the Christian gospel. Not everything we read in the biblical stories reflects the values of the Christian gospel, such as for instance the violence, slavery, gender inequality and social injustice we encounter. Those sections of the Bible tell us something about the spiritual journey of God's people in the past, but do not always adequately reflect the character of God and are often at variance with the life that Christ has modeled for us. Therefore, these parts of the Bible must not determine our way of thinking, our faith and our life.

This is where the second 'pole' comes in. The Bible was written in a particular cultural context. The authors were embedded in an ancient culture. Much of the Bible reflects a patriarchal society with cultural norms and customs that can no longer be normative for us. So, when we read the Bible we must constantly be aware of these cultural influences and try to separate the essential message of the Bible, and the principles it contains, from the cultural packaging. This is not easy for many Adventists, and certainly not for those who advocate a 'plain' reading of the Bible and silence every argument by a simplistic 'the Bible says...'

The third pole in our approach to the Bible is our Adventist heritage. As I said earlier, we read the Bible through Adventist spectacles. This is not, in itself, something totally negative. Adventists of the past bring a rich heritage to the table, with insights that we must gratefully acknowledge. We never start as a *tabula rasa* (a clean slate) but always stand on the shoulders of our forebears. I realize that much of my theological thinking has been deeply influenced by a number of Adventist scholars whom I hold in high esteem. But our Adventist heritage is just one of the three poles and must not overrule the other two. While our Adventist heritage must not be denied or belittled, we must always be aware that it influences our thinking and we must realize that it may not only clarify things for us but at times also cause distortions that we must identify and correct.

ELLEN G. WHITE

One issue that also needs careful reflection is our attitude towards Ellen G. White. I would be the last person to say that she no longer has any importance for the Seventh-day Adventist Church. On the other hand, I can understand the problems many Adventist 'believers on the margins' have with the way she is often put on a pedestal and with the way many use her writings as the last word that can solve every issue. It is high time that the person and work of Ellen White are further demythologized.

When Ellen White died in 1915 her status was not as elevated as it is in many quarters of the church today. In fact, for a number of years the leaders of the church resisted the plans of William White, the oldest son of Ellen, to publish any of the materials she left behind in unpublished manuscript form.[8] Later, in the 1920s and the 1930s, the tide began to turn. A more fundamentalist view of inspiration gained increasing support in the church and this affected the way in which the writings of Ellen White were viewed. This change in attitude led, among other things, to the production of an extensive range of 'compilations,' that is, of collections of quotes from all across her writings (often without due regard for context) of what she had written about particular topics.[9]

As more books by Ellen White were published, translated into many different languages and strongly promoted, the role of 'the prophet' became ever more pronounced. Even in parts of Europe where there had long been considerable reluctance with regard to this trend— notably from such leaders as Ludwig Conradi—the situation changed.

In my own country, the Netherlands, pastors had traditionally been trained in Germany, but after World War II they went to Newbold College in England, where Ellen G. White was attributed a much more important role.

This development in the church did not go unchallenged. In 1976 historian Ronald Numbers dropped a stone in the Adventist pond, which sent waves across the world. The book remained influential, in spite of strenuous efforts of the church's leadership at damage control. Numbers placed Ellen White's views of health in the context of the nineteenth century and provided convincing evidence that most of her counsels on healthful living and simple natural remedies were not as unique as had hitherto been claimed. In fact, much of what she wrote and promoted was clearly inspired by other 'health reformers' of that time.[10] A new shock, which was more than a stone in the Adventist pond, but might be compared to a 'tsunami' in the sea of Adventism, was a book by former Adventist pastor Walter Rea. He presented undeniable evidence that Ellen G. White had borrowed heavily from other authors, often copying lengthy sections, without mentioning her sources.[11] Other 'discoveries' followed this charge of plagiarism. Donald R. McAdams, for instance, focused in a detailed study on the historical errors in some E.G. White books, as for instance in *The Great Controversy*.[12]

The Ellen G. White Estate—the organization that is responsible for the custody of the literary heritage of Ellen White—did what it could to take the sting out of these damaging revelations. It also came with (in my view not always completely successful) responses to difficult questions that were being raised about some very unusual statements made by Ellen White. At the same time other authors wanted to uphold her authority and importance, but put more stress on the human side of the prophet than was often done before.[13] I found two recent books very helpful in getting a more realistic picture of Ellen White. Gilbert Valentine investigated the dynamics in the relationships between Ellen G. White and three General Conference presidents. It clearly shows how Ellen White had strong opinions about their suitability for their office, and how she was at times quite political, or even manipulative, in her dealings with them.[14] Another book, with essays by eighteen Adventist and non-Adventist scholars, deals, on a more academic level, with many aspects of the person and work of Ellen White. It provides information about her that was little known, or even completely unknown, until now.[15] A response to this and other recent books, which was coordinated by the White Estate, shows that the church apparently feels that the research of scholars who have highlighted different problematic issues should not go unanswered.[16] It is all part of a process that will, no doubt, continue.

Adventist 'believers on the margins' would do well to read some of the books that I have mentioned or referred to in the footnotes. They will help to give a more balanced view of Ellen White and to appreciate more fully that she lived and wrote in the nineteenth century American world. Many of the principles that she emphasized are still valuable for us today. But as we read her books we should not forget that she wrote in the Victorian age, and was subject to the limitations in scientific knowledge of that period. Moreover, she was not a trained historian or theologian. Her historical references are not watertight and her use of the Bible mostly followed a proof-text approach. The language she used is rather cumbersome for many of us today, and we can hardly expect that young people, in particular, will flock to her writings in great numbers. All this does not mean that her writings are no longer of any use for Adventists today, but we should not look for more in them than we can reasonably expect. As Adventists we do well to treasure her complete books (rather than the so-called compilations) as devotional reading for the enrichment of our spiritual life.

In biblical times many prophets spoke on behalf of God. Some of them are merely mentioned in the Bible in passing and even a few of the 'great' prophets, such as Elijah and Elisha, have left us no writings. On the other hand, the prophets who have contributed writings to the Bible may have written more than we have in our biblical canon today. Over time a selection was made and the biblical canon was established. This must, I think, give us some direction with regard to the writings of Ellen G. White. Time will do its work and gradually some kind of consensus may emerge about what should be seen as the core of what she wrote. It would seem to me that such books as *Steps to Christ*, *The Desire of Ages* and *Christ's Object Lessons* would be at, or near, the top of the list. 'Believers on the margins' who want to get a good taste of what she wrote may want to start with these or similar books.

PRAY

I hope my remarks about our Bible reading, the role of our thoughtful reflection, and my comments on the place of Ellen G. White in Adventism have been helpful. It is important, however, to make sure that all of this does not remain too much on a purely cerebral level. Included in our 'leap of faith' is the expectation that God wants to communicate with us. Christians would say that he does this through his Spirit. Again, we will leave complicated theological issues relating to the Person and the work of the Holy Spirit aside. In connection with what we are discussing in this chapter I want to underline that we can only receive full spiritual benefit from our Bible reading and from the thinking we may do about what we read, if we allow God somehow to tell us what we should focus on and how this might relate to our life in the here and now. Prayer is the usual word for this act of opening ourselves up to this divine influence.

For many believers—and not only for those 'on the margins'—prayer does not come easy. When we have tried to pray, many of our prayers may have remained empty formulas and flowed from habit rather than from conviction. It is often not easy to find the right words to express our deepest feelings and motives. Even Jesus' disciples wondered how they should pray and asked, 'Teach us how to pray' (Luke 11:1). In answer to their request Jesus gave them the so-called 'Lord's Prayer' (Our Father, who is in heaven...). In addition to our 'leap of faith' we may also need to take a 'leap of trust' and expect God to hear us when we pray for guidance.[17]

If you are not in the habit of praying, or do not know how to pray, repeating the words of the 'Lord's Prayer' may be a good start. Or, when you have read a section from the Bible, interrupt your thinking about the possible meaning these texts have for you, and just say, 'God, help me to discover what I need to see and to find answers to my questions,' and then just be quiet for a few moments. In other words, give God the opportunity to communicate with you and to point you to things that are important for you and that may answer some of your questions.

So, *talk with God* about your doubts and ask him for guidance as you are searching for answers. In addition, *talk with other people.* It is important to be selective in who you talk to about your uncertainties and doubts. Some people in your local church or elsewhere will only become confused if they know what you are struggling with, and that is not going to help you or them. But, if you look carefully, you will always find people who have similar experiences to yours and who will be grateful if you want to share your thoughts and questions with them. In many cases it will help them and also yourself to talk together. There may be a friend, a pastor or elder who can be a guide— someone who can lead you to some new thoughts, or point you to some biblical passages that may inspire 'people on the margins' like you, or suggest a book that might stimulate your thinking. And you may find someone who has travelled along a similar path, but is slightly ahead of you, and who has been able to take the right course when faced with 'Spaghetti Junctions'[18] and, as a result, can help you in resetting your spiritual GPS.

'QUESTIONS ON DOCTRINES'

Sooner or later Adventist 'believers on the margins' must face their doubts with regard to various specific doctrines of their church. In addition to what I said in the previous chapter about ranking doctrines with respect to their relative importance, and in reaction to the question how many doctrines a 'real' Adventist must minimally embrace, I here want to reemphasize one further point. We should not be afraid to ask critical questions with regard to the way in which the Adventist tradition has defined and formulated some of our teachings. Roy Adams, a former editor of the *Adventist Review,* who tried to open up the discussion about details of the traditional sanctuary doctrine, took issue with people who think 'that the positions we have held on every doctrine or theological issue should remain frozen in formaldehyde forever—never to be examined again, never to be modified, never to be refined.'[19] The same author quoted the following intriguing statement at the beginning of his doctoral dissertation on the Adventist understanding of the doctrine of the heavenly sanctuary: 'Great philosophical or theological issues are seldom resolved to the satisfaction of succeeding generations.'[20] I fully share this sentiment. It gives me breathing space and a sense of freedom to look anew at the doctrines of my church in an open and critical manner.

I am not for a moment suggesting that approaching doubts in the way that I have described is easy. I know of no quick fix. But some of the things I have said may help you to find the inner peace that you need while facing your doubts and looking for answers. One important ingredient in this process is time. We must not be in too much of a hurry in dealing with our doubts. Often doubts have grown over many years and it may take just as long for the dust of doubt to be settled. I have found it very useful to focus on just one of the issues that have troubled me for a long period of time, while locking away my other doubts in a cupboard with a strong padlock. When after much reading, thinking and prayer—and often many helpful discussions with others—I have found some answers to a specific issue, I allow myself to retrieve another topic from my cupboard. I have found that this makes my doubts manageable. When I try to deal with all my questions at one and the same time, it just leaves me stressed out. It creates panic, and I am left with a sense that everything may be up for grabs and nothing is certain anymore.

Os Guinness has made some helpful comments when he discussed the life of the believer as that of a pilgrim at a 'Spaghetti Junction'— as someone who must constantly choose what road to take when so many options present themselves.[21] He warns us that finding answers for our doubts is not like passing a simple crossroads and that is why he compares our search with passing through a 'Spaghetti Junction.'

Guinness suggests there are four phases in our journey towards being a balanced Christian believer.

First there is the time for questions. (I believe we have taken ample time for that phase in the first five chapters of this book.) It means we must become a seeker, and be willing, if necessary, to let go of previous ideas, and be open to other views.

In *phase two* we are looking for answers. We consider potential alternatives to replace or modify the views we have earlier held but are no longer certain about.

Phase three Guinness calls the phase of evidence; we test our new insights and try to determine how they might fit into the larger framework of our religious convictions. For Adventists this means that we determine how we can make these new ideas, which we feel comfortable with, fit into our framework of Adventism and how we may become or remain 'real' Adventists—even though we may deviate from some (or many) traditional Adventist viewpoints.

We have tried to contribute to phases two and three in the second part of this book. But, Guinness says, do not forget the *final phase*, which is the most important one. After having gone through the three phases comes the time for (re)-commitment; ensuring that our new insights have a concrete impact on our daily lives. For, after all, that is what really counts.

In 1998 the Pacific Press Publishing Association published a small book that I had written about the (then) twenty-seven *Fundamental Beliefs*.[22] It was quite simple and did not contain any deep theology. I looked briefly at each of the *Fundamental Beliefs* and in each case asked myself the question, What difference does it actually make that I believe this? I started with the premise that 'truth' must *do* something for me. Christ told his audience that the truth would 'set them free' (John 8:32). The truth is not a theory, a philosophical or theological system, but a change agent that must transform people. So, going through all the twenty-seven points I asked myself, How does believing this particular doctrine make me a better, more balanced, more pleasant and more spiritual human being? If it does not do something for me, it has no real value.

To my surprise nothing that I wrote before or since brought me so many positive reactions. This little book seemed to strike a chord with many readers. Like me, they also wanted to believe in something that actually impacts on our life—that is relevant or, to use a traditional Adventist expression, something that is 'present truth.'

MY JOURNEY

I do not have to claim the prophetic gift to say that I am closer to the end of my life than to its beginning. Once people are retired they begin to feel the tendency to look back at what is in their past. At the beginning of my ministry I could probably have been described as a fundamentalist. But throughout my life I have always asked questions. And I have found answers to many of them. I have changed my views on many things and gradually I have experienced a theological shift. Some would now call me a 'liberal,' while others have called me a 'progressive' Adventist. (I like that second label better!) However, I do not like to be put in a particular box. Maybe I can summarize my spiritual journey best by saying that I have always tried to be an independent thinker, but at the same time I have consistently tried to be loyal to my Lord, my church and myself.

If I were to give a summary of where I am at present in my journey as a Christian and as an Adventist, and were asked to state the main content of what I believe, my personal statement of *Fundamental Beliefs* would look something like this:

I BELIEVE
- that God is three in one: Father, Son and Holy Spirit.
- that God is the Creator of everything, and that, therefore, I am a created being with the privileges and responsibilities this implies.
- that Jesus Christ came to our earth and has radically solved the sin problem through his death and resurrection—for the world and for me.
- that the Holy Spirit guides my conscience and has equipped me with certain gifts, so that I may serve God better.
- that the Bible is an inspired book that tells the story of God's involvement with humankind, and provides me with basic guiding principles, so that I can try to live as God intended.

- that, as a human being, I am subject to death, but that, when I die, my identity is somehow safe with God; and that he will give me a new start in an eternal existence.
- that our present world is infected by evil of demonic proportions, so that a solution is needed from on high; Christ will complete this process when he returns to this earth and creates a 'new heaven and a new earth.'
- that as a follower of Christ I can only live authentically if I consciously seek to shape my life after the principles he has modeled for me.
- that every seventh-day Sabbath I have the unique opportunity to experience the rest that God provides.
- that I am responsible for how I use the resources of this earth and how I use my time, my material means, and my talents, and for how I treat my body.
- that, together with all true Christians, I can be a member of God's church.
- that the faith community to which I belong has an important part in the worldwide proclamation of the gospel and has the task of placing a number of important accents.
- that through my baptism I may be part of God's church and can, in celebrating the Lord's Supper, be regularly reminded of Christ's suffering and death.
- that I may experience spiritual growth together with those in the community of which I feel a part.

Of course, such a list of 'fundamentals' can never be final. And it should be noted that what I have listed is 'fundamental' for *me*. Others will have to reflect on what is 'fundamental' for *them*, and will probably use different words, add certain points, or leave out certain elements.

This is the crux of the matter: It is good to reflect from time to time on what is really 'fundamental' in our faith. It helps to differentiate between primary and secondary things and not to treat secondary things as if they are the most important.

Having reached the last paragraph of this book I can tell you who read it that writing it has been good for my own soul. I earnestly hope that it will give many of you, who are 'believers on the margins,' a handle on your questions and your doubts; that it may rekindle an experience of living faith, and help you to move away from 'the margins' of the church and find a blessing in more fully participating in your faith community.

I know that the Adventist faith community is far from perfect. But God is putting up with it—and so should we.

1   Nathan Brown, op. cit., p. 38.
2   Ibid. p. 41.
3   Ibid.
4   Published by Maryknoll in New York, NY, 2002.
5   Ibid., back cover.
6   Os Guinness, 'Pilgrim at the Spaghetti Junction: An Evangelical Perspective on Relativism and Fundamentalism,' in: Peter L. Berger, ed., *Between Relativism and Fundamentalism* (Grand Rapids, MI: Wm. B. Eerdmans Publishing Company, 2010), p. 171.
7   Fritz Guy, op. cit., pp. 225-252.
8   The story of the conflict between William White and his family and the General Conference leaders is described in a meticulously researched book by Gilbert Valentine: *The Struggle for the Prophetic Heritage* (Muak Lek, Thailand: Institute Press, 2006).
9   A few of the many compilations are, e.g.: *Messages to Young People, Counsels on Diet and Food, Counsels on Sabbath School Work, Counsels to Writers and Editors.*
10 Ronald L. Numbers, *Prophetess of Health: A Study of Ellen G. White* (New York: Harper & Row, 1976).
11 Walter Rea, The White Lie (Turlock, CA: M & R Publications, 1982).
12 See: https://archive.org/stream/DonaldR.McadamsShiftingViewsOfInspiration EllenWhiteStudiesInThe/1980_mcadams_shiftingViewsOfInspiration_ellen WhiteStudiesInThe1970s_spectrum_v10_n4_27-41_djvu.txt
13 As, for instance George R. Knight with his popular books: *Walking with Ellen White* (Hagerstown: Review and Herald, 2000); and *Reading Ellen White* (Hagerstown: Review and Herald, 2001). Also Graeme Bradford, *Prophets are Human* (Warburton, Australia: Signs Publishing House, 2004) and *People are Human (Look what they did to Ellen White)*, (Warburton, Australia: Signs Publishing House, 2006).
14 Gilbert M. Valentine, *The Prophet and the Presidents* (Nampa, ID: Pacific Press, 2011).

15 Terry Dopp Aamodt et. al., eds., *Ellen Harmon White: American Prophet* (New York, NY: Oxford University Press, 2014).

16 Merlin D. Burt, ed., *Understanding Ellen White* (Nampa, ID: Pacific Press, 2015).

17 Philip Yancey, *Prayer. Does it Make any Difference?* (Grand Rapids, MI: Zondervan, 2006), p. 209.

18 See p. 187.

19 Roy Adams, 'Sanctuary' in: Gary Chartier, ed.: *The Future of Adventism: Theology, Society. Experience* (Ann Arbor, MI: Griffin & Lash, Publishers, 2015), p. 143.

20 Ibid., p. 154.

21 'Pilgrim at the Spaghetti Junction: An Evangelical Perspective on Relativism and Fundamentalism' in: Peter L. Berger, op. cit., pp. 164-179.

22 Reinder Bruinsma, *It's Time to Stop Rehearsing What We Believe and Start Looking at What Difference It Makes* (Nampa, ID: Pacific Press, 1996).